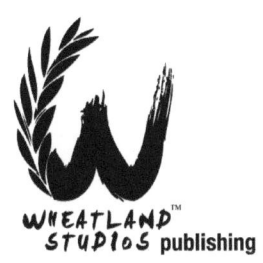

Copyright © 2018
by Matthew J. Spencer

All rights reserved. No part of this book may be reproduced or used in any manner without written permission.

First printed on Blurb May 2018

Book design by Matthew J. Spencer

Created at Wheatland Studios™
LONGMONT, COLORADO

ISBN used on CreateSpace:
9781719281829

Published by Wheatland Studios™ Publishing

A Spencers Unleashed™ Product

www.MatthewSpencer.TV

Titles of Pieces in Order of Appearance:

Mediterranean Fishing Boat
Toucan
Austrian Church
City Park
Pony Canyon
Volcano Sky
Underwater
Volcano
Longs Peak (Pen & Ink)
Longs Peak (Watercolor Only)
Longs Peak Nightscape
Longs Peak From the Front Range
Longs Peak Vineyard
Smoke Bombs
Cartoon Flamingo
Cartoon Kookaburra
Desert
African Savannah
Bamboo Hut
New Wavelength
Horse & Lion
Weather Gun
Candle Hut
Tranquility Base
Tranquility Base Space Dock
Lions By Moonlight
Watchmen On the Wall
Landing Site
Toucan Flying
Pig
Planets Compass
Spaceship Rainforest Landing
Space Ship City
Sun Bird
Dude with Glasses
Firebird Sunset
Multicultural Man
Matthew Self-Portrait
Self-Portrait with Watercolors on Mirror

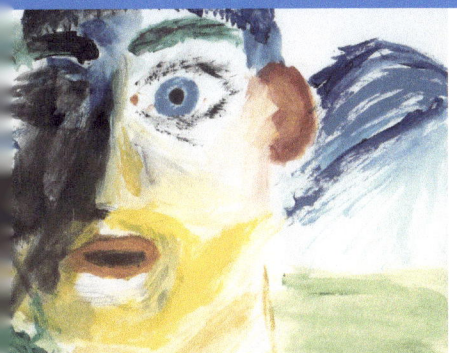
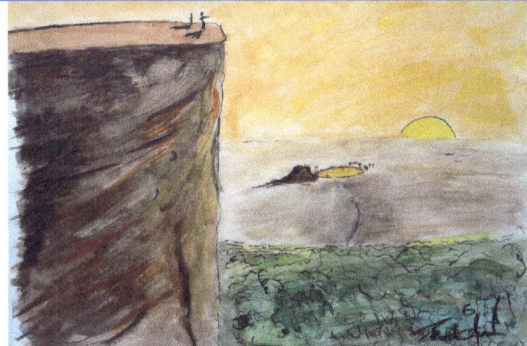
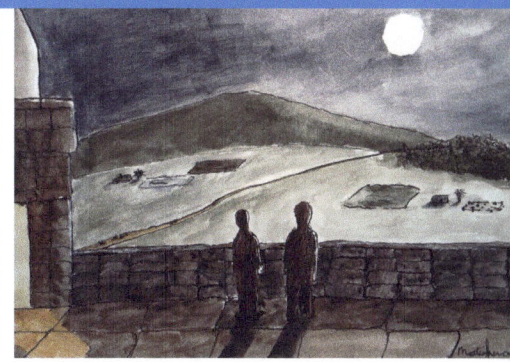
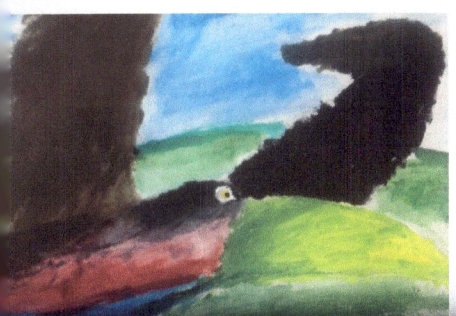
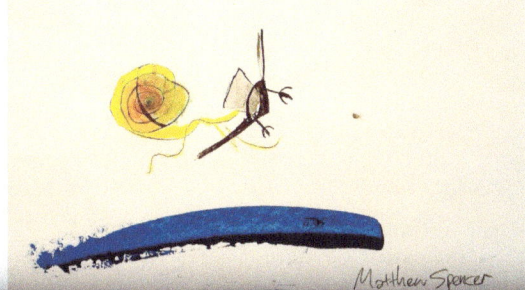
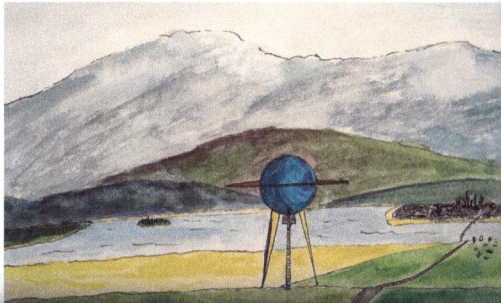

Watercolors
Volume 1

Matthew Spencer

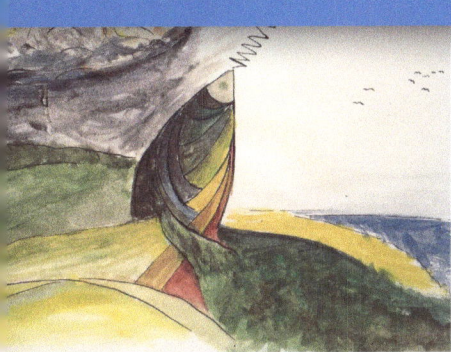
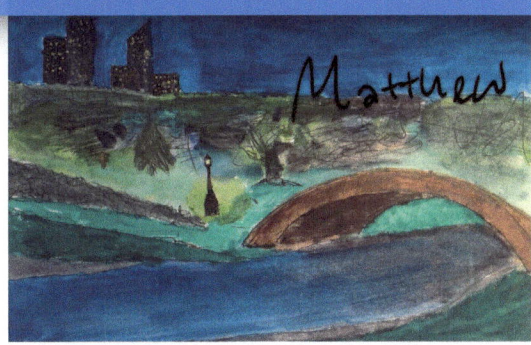
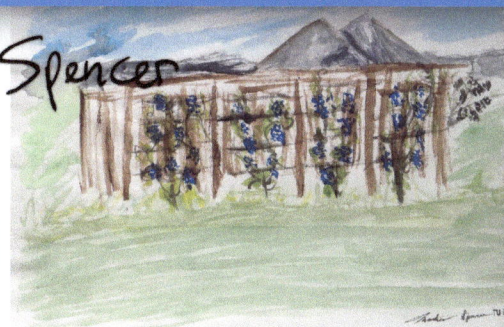
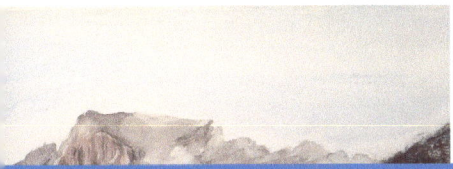
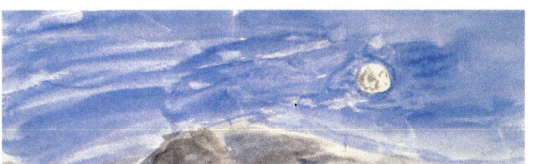
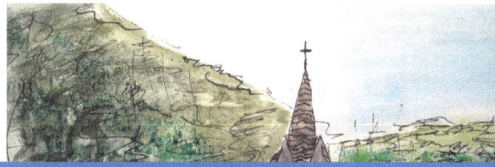

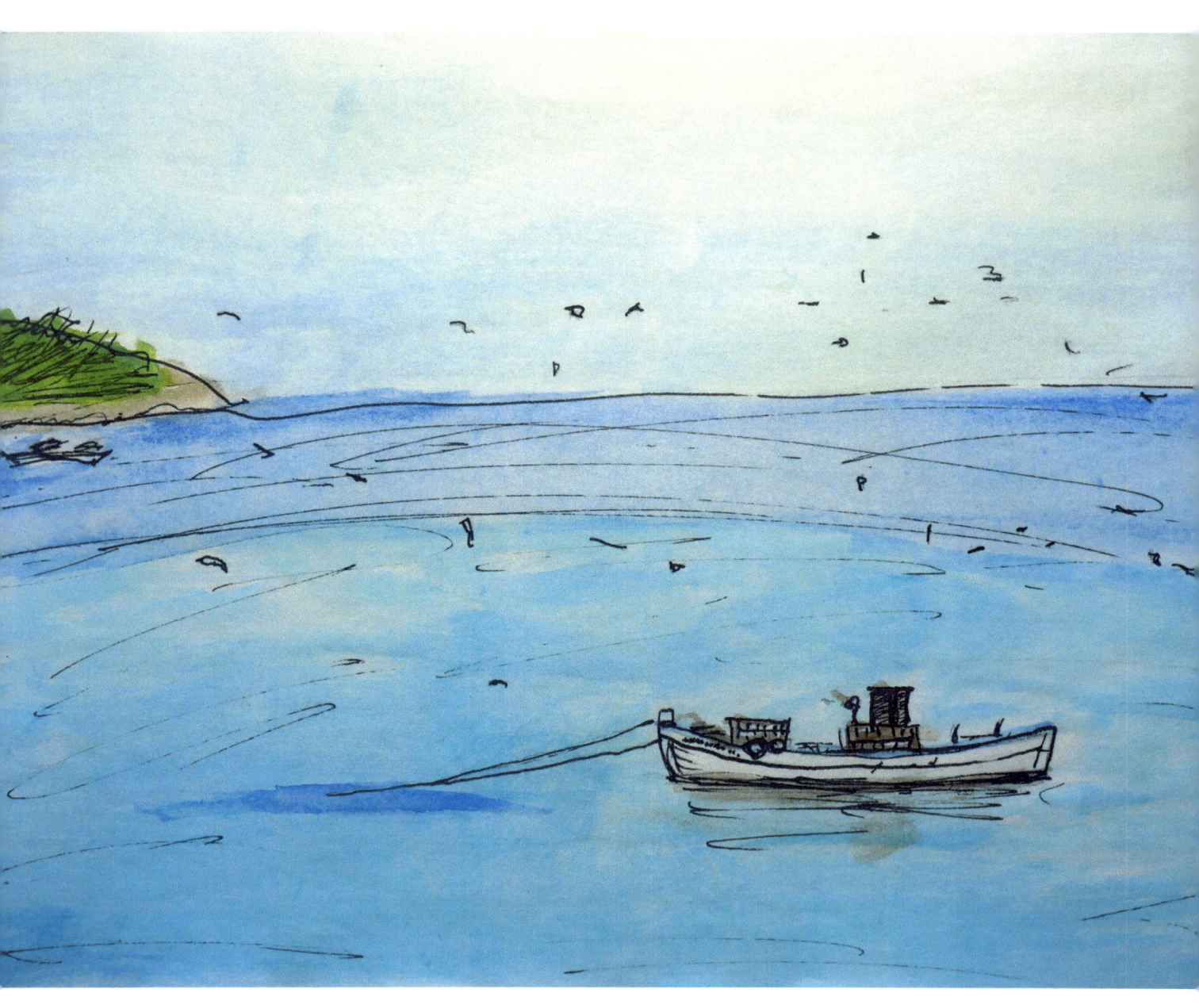

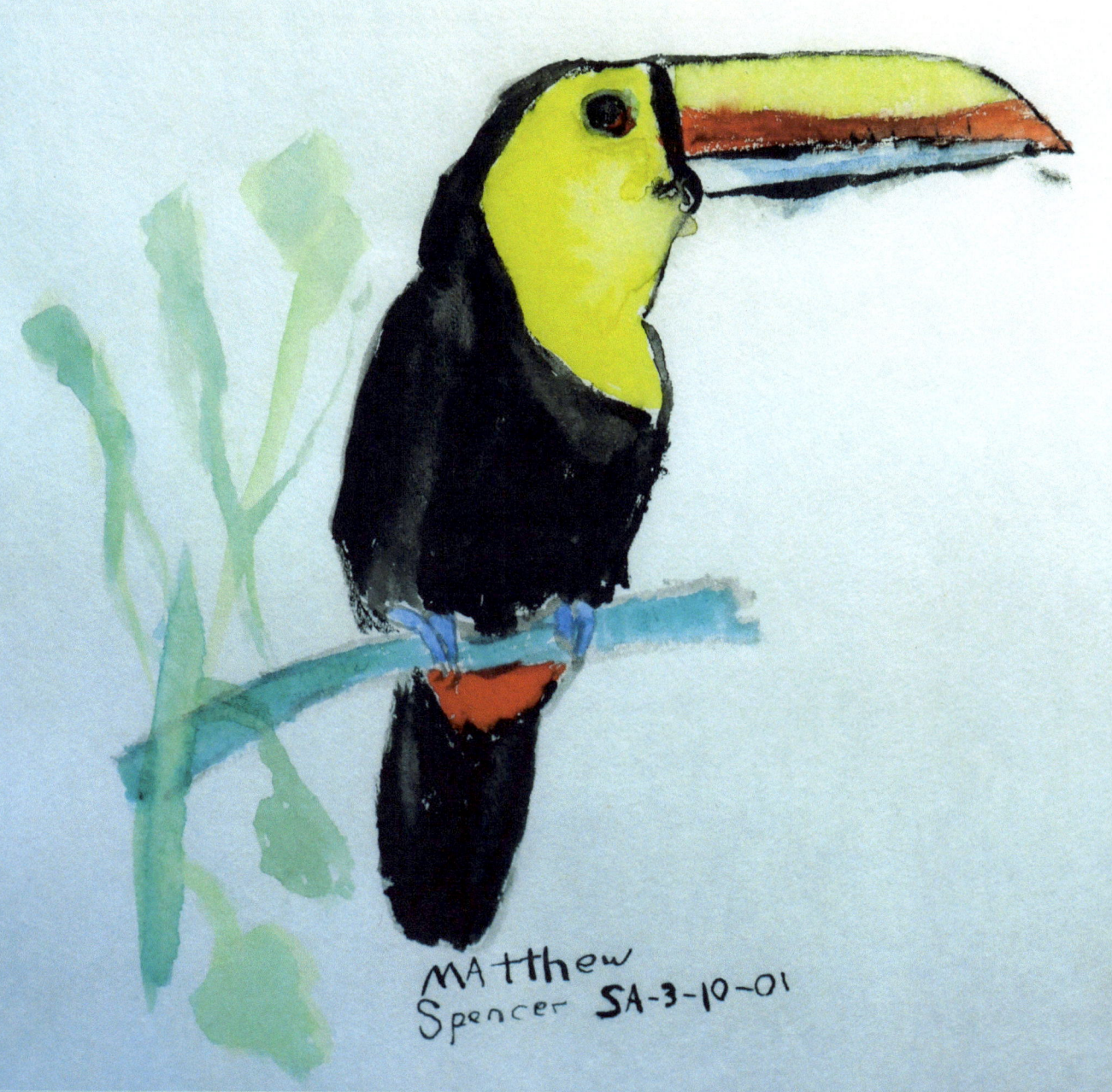

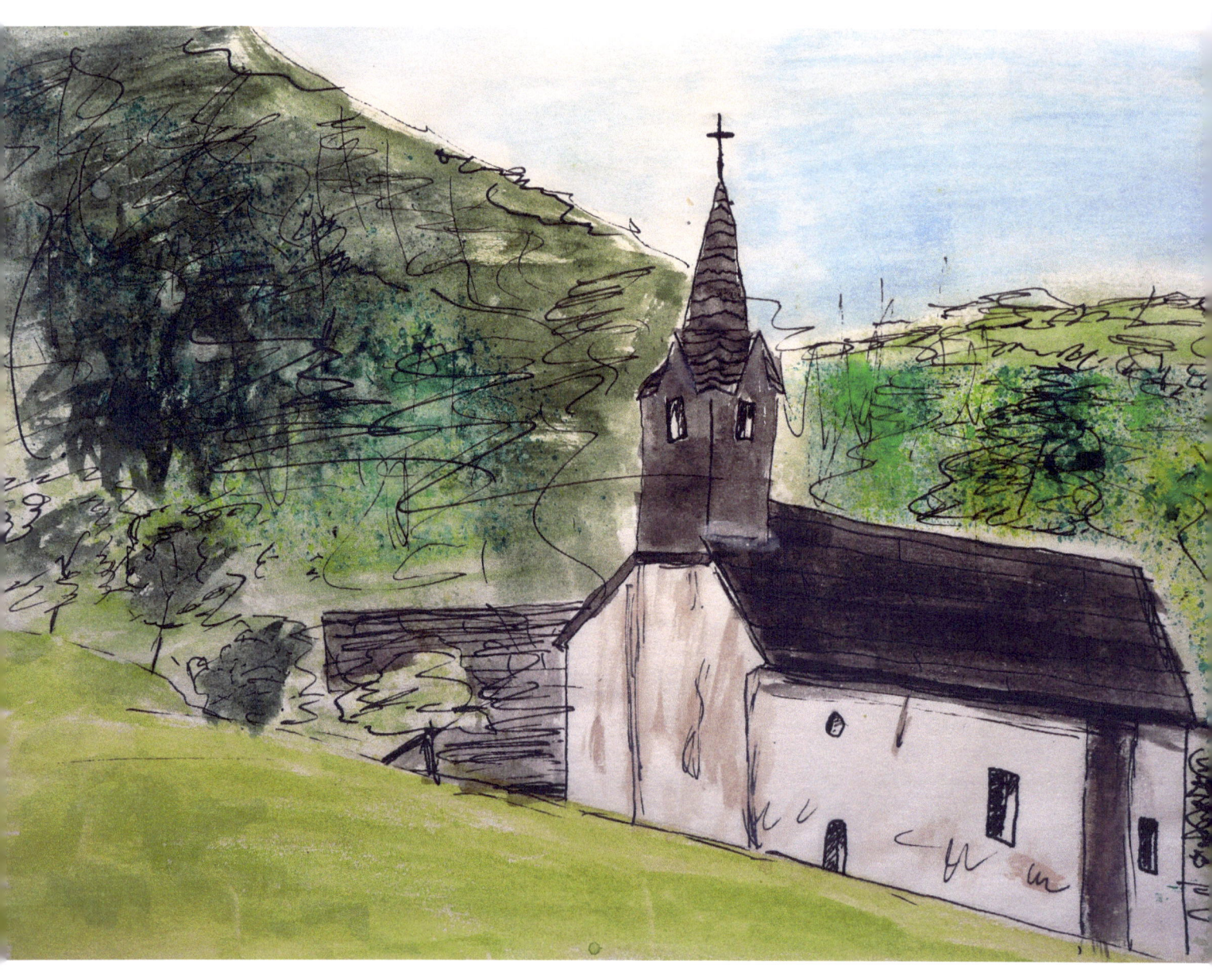

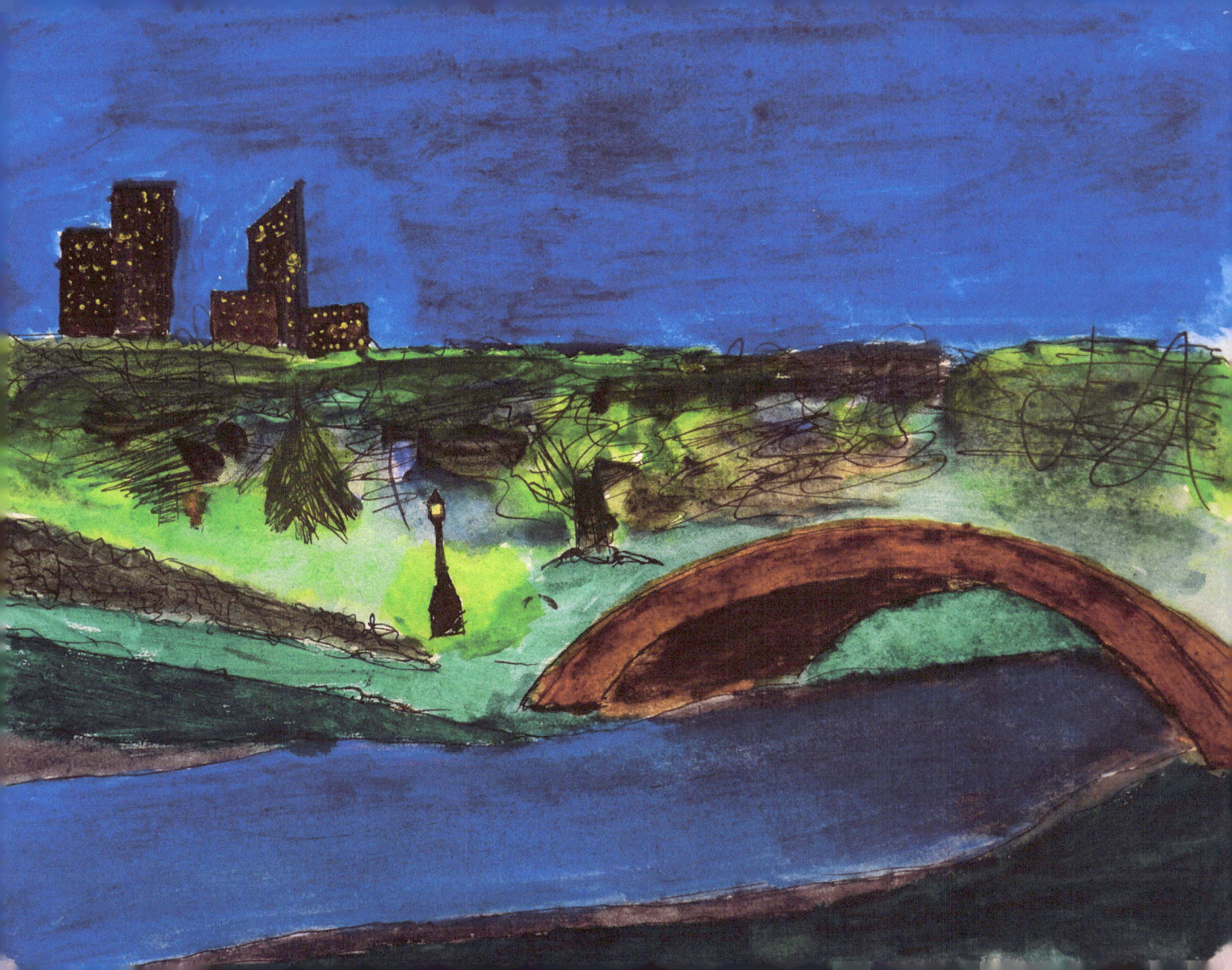

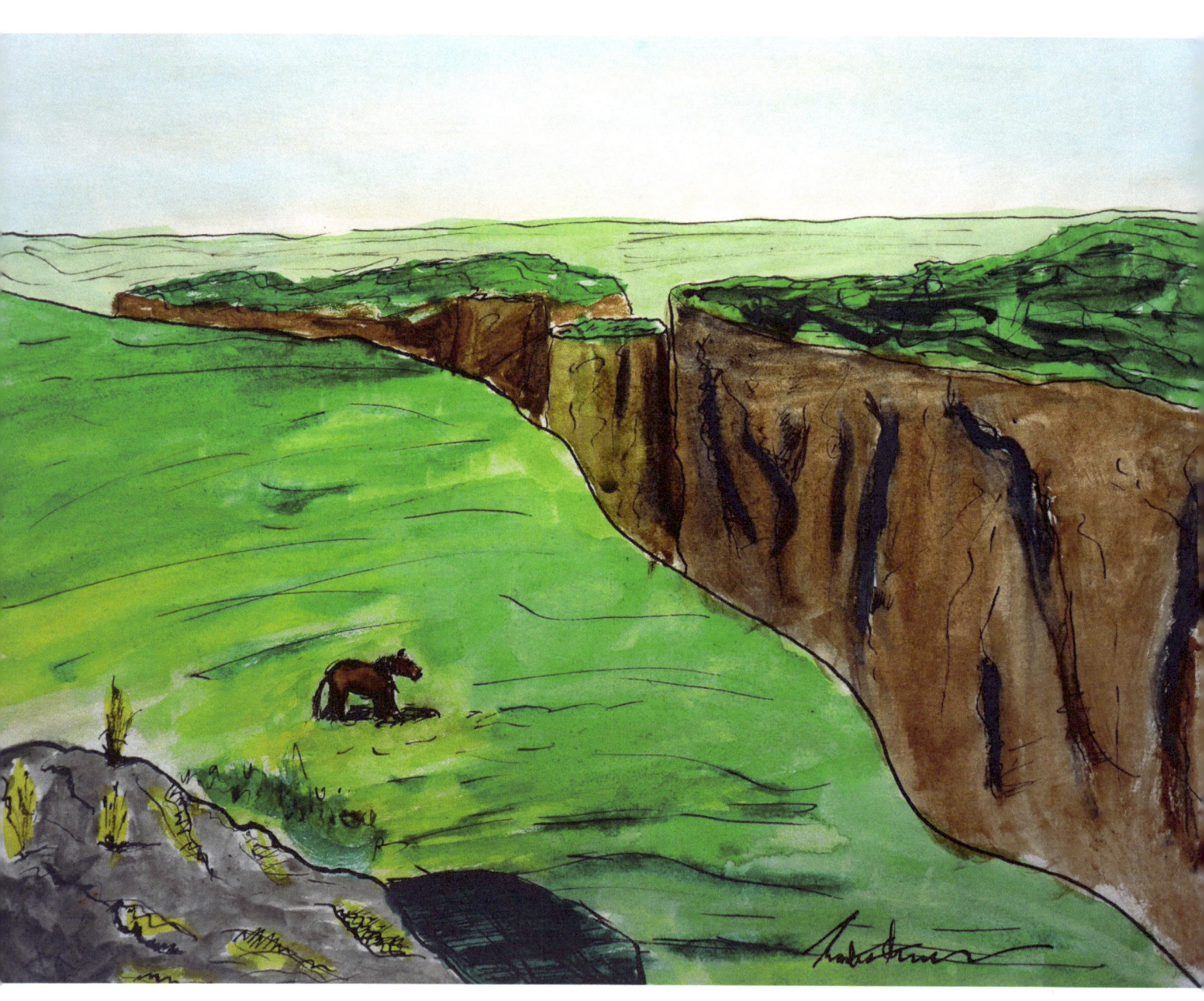

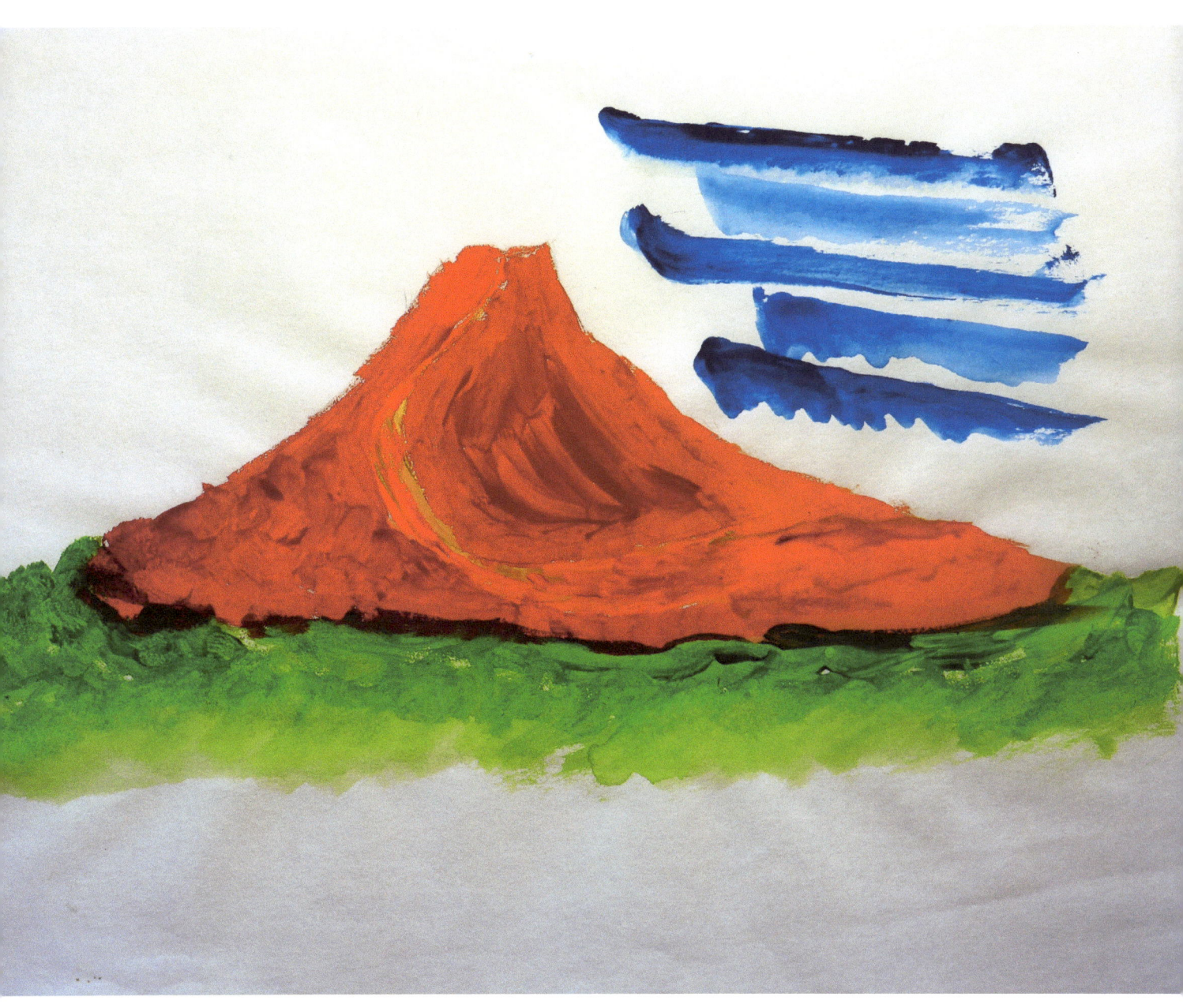

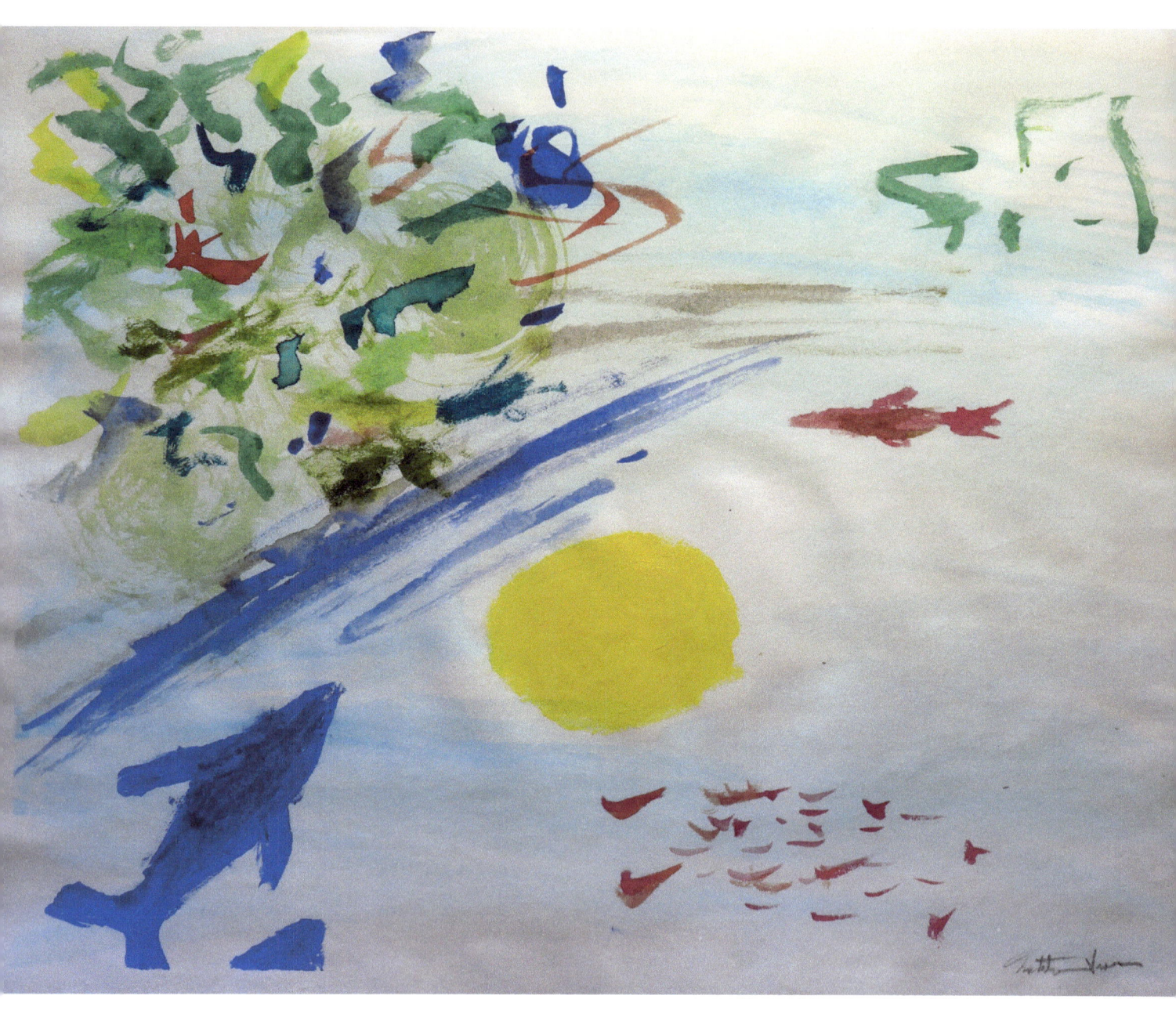

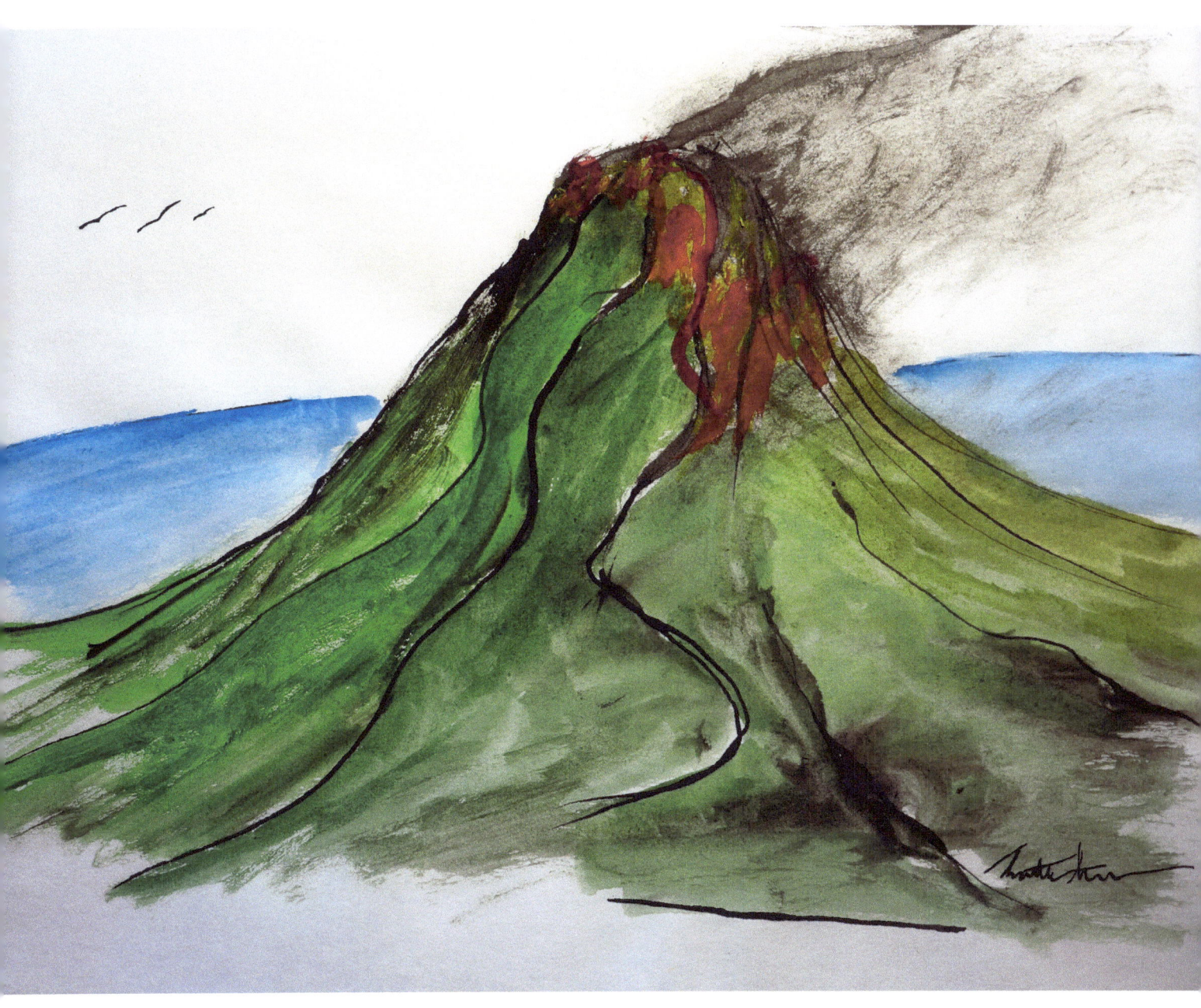

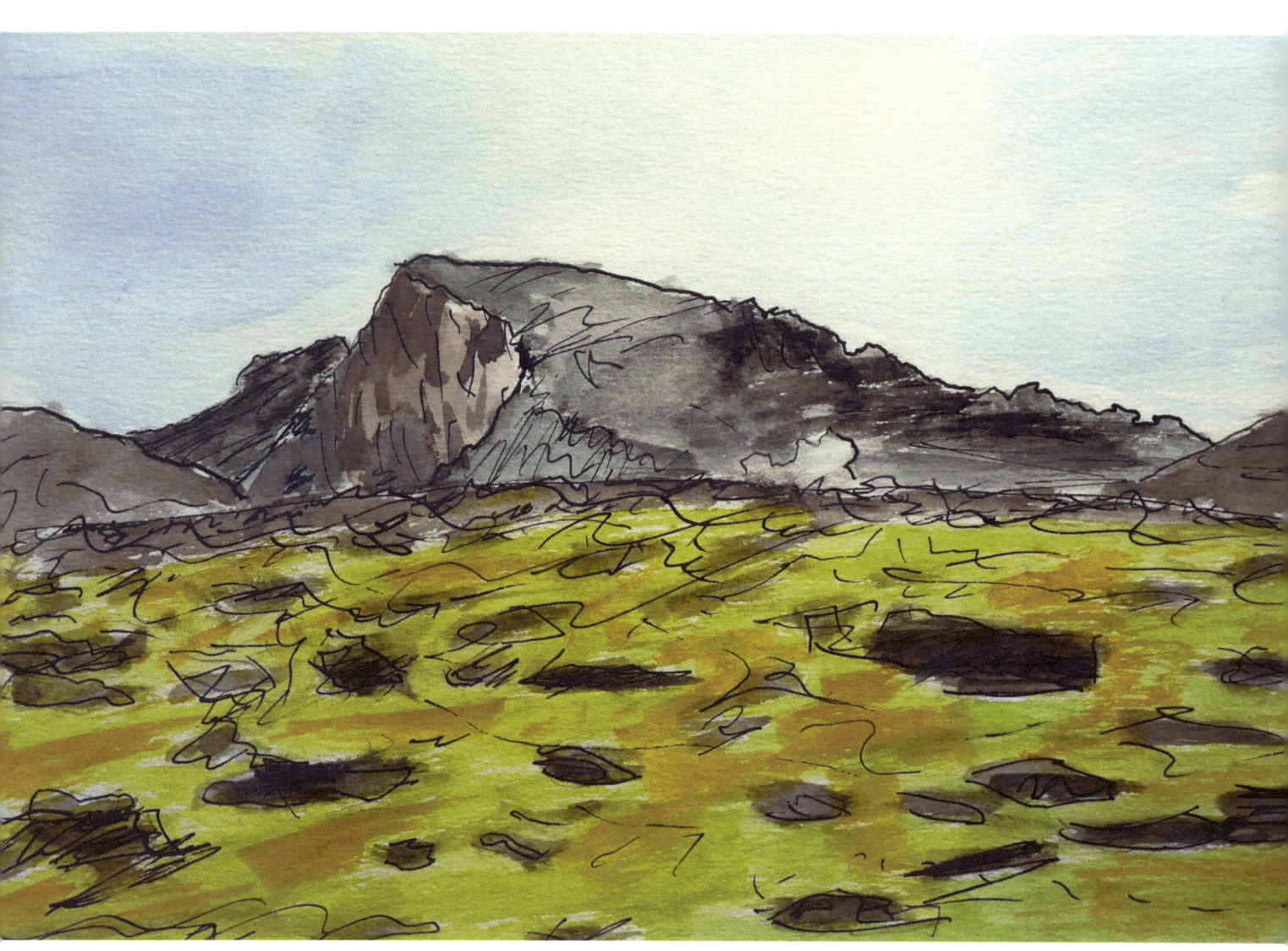

Inspired by the experience of hiking Longs Peak, Matthew did three watercolors afterwards from the perspective of the Longs Peak Boulderfield. One is pen & ink, one watercolor only, and one a nightscape.

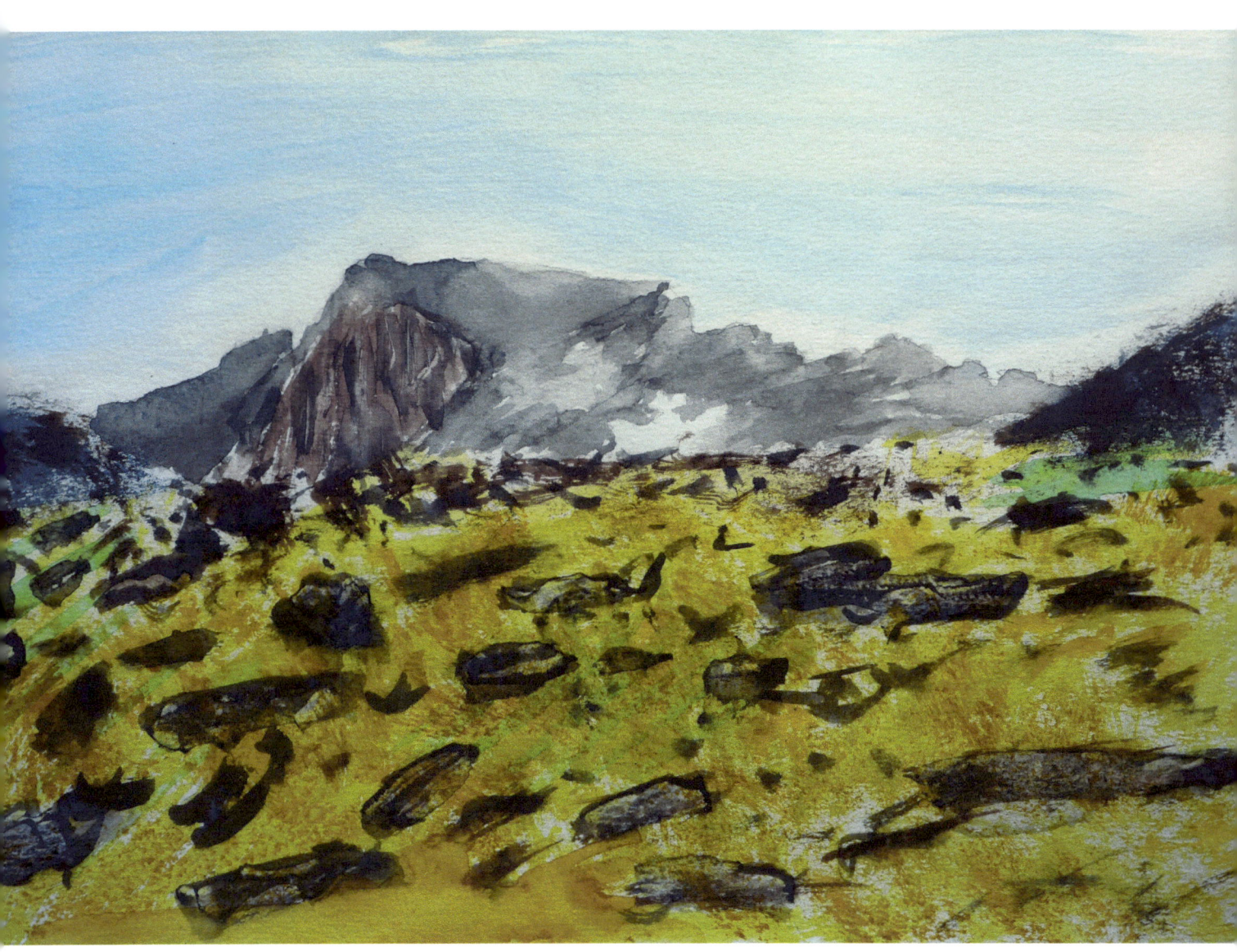

Longs Peak Watercolor Only

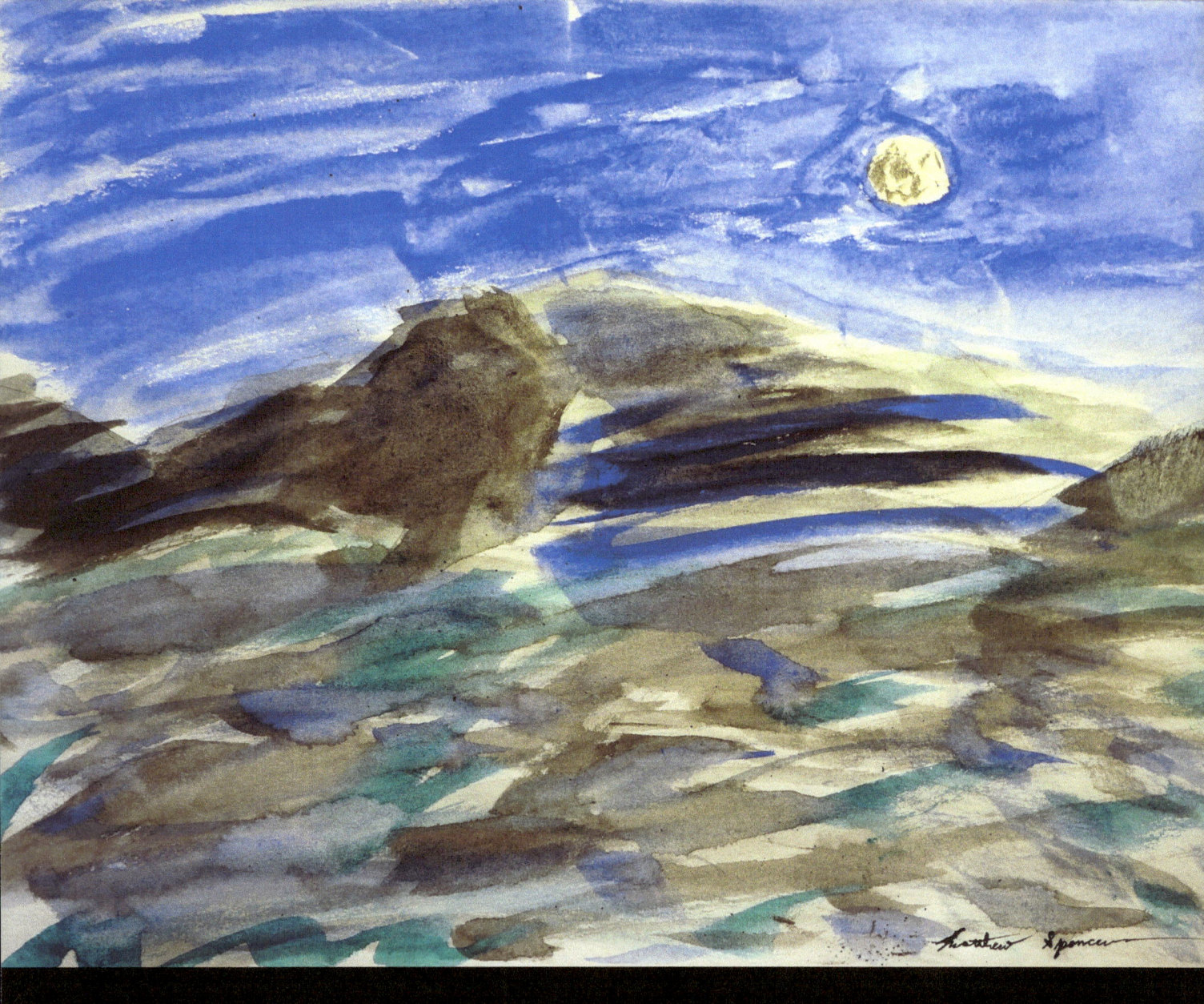

Longs Peak Nightscape

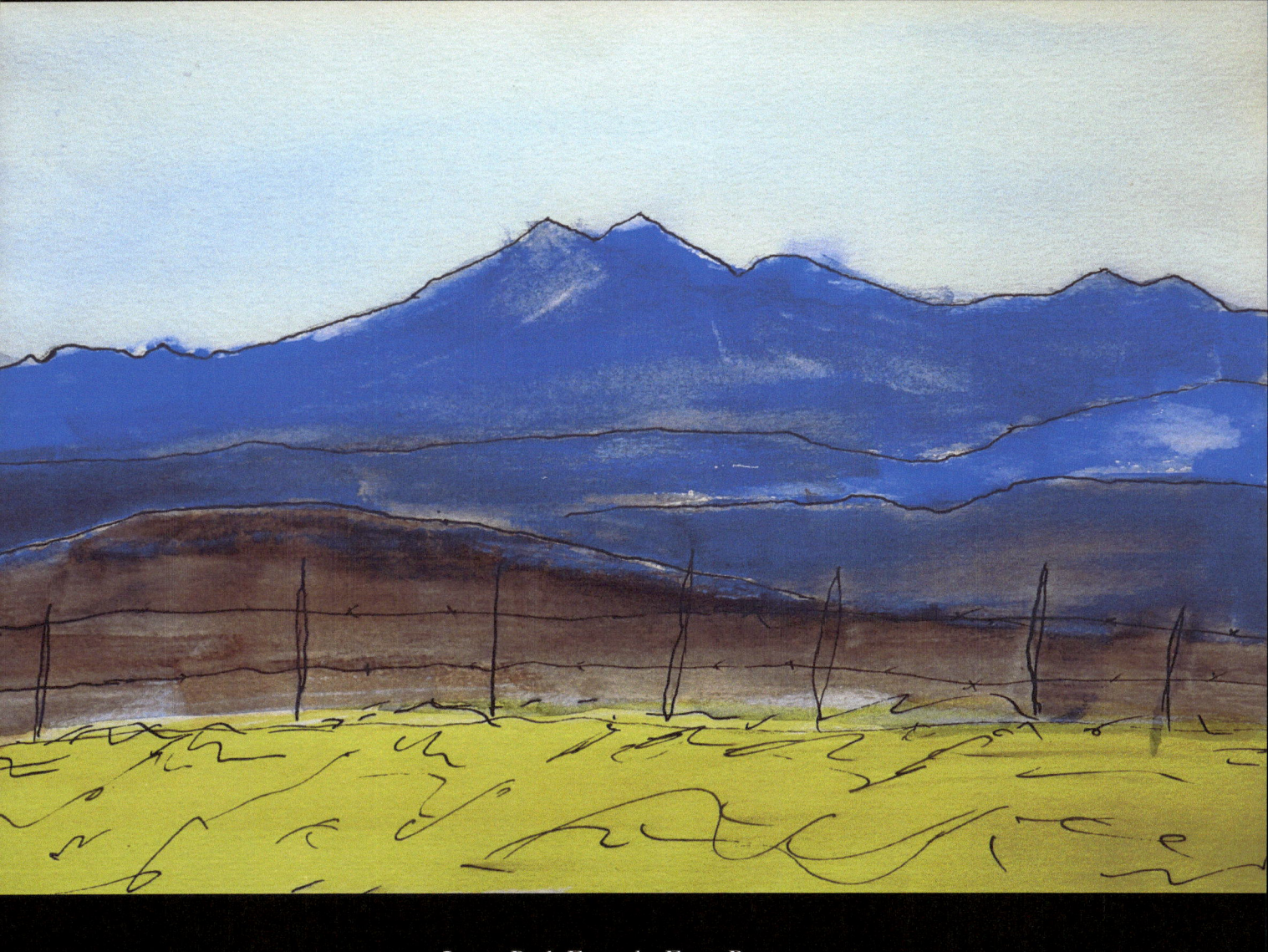
Longs Peak From the Front Range

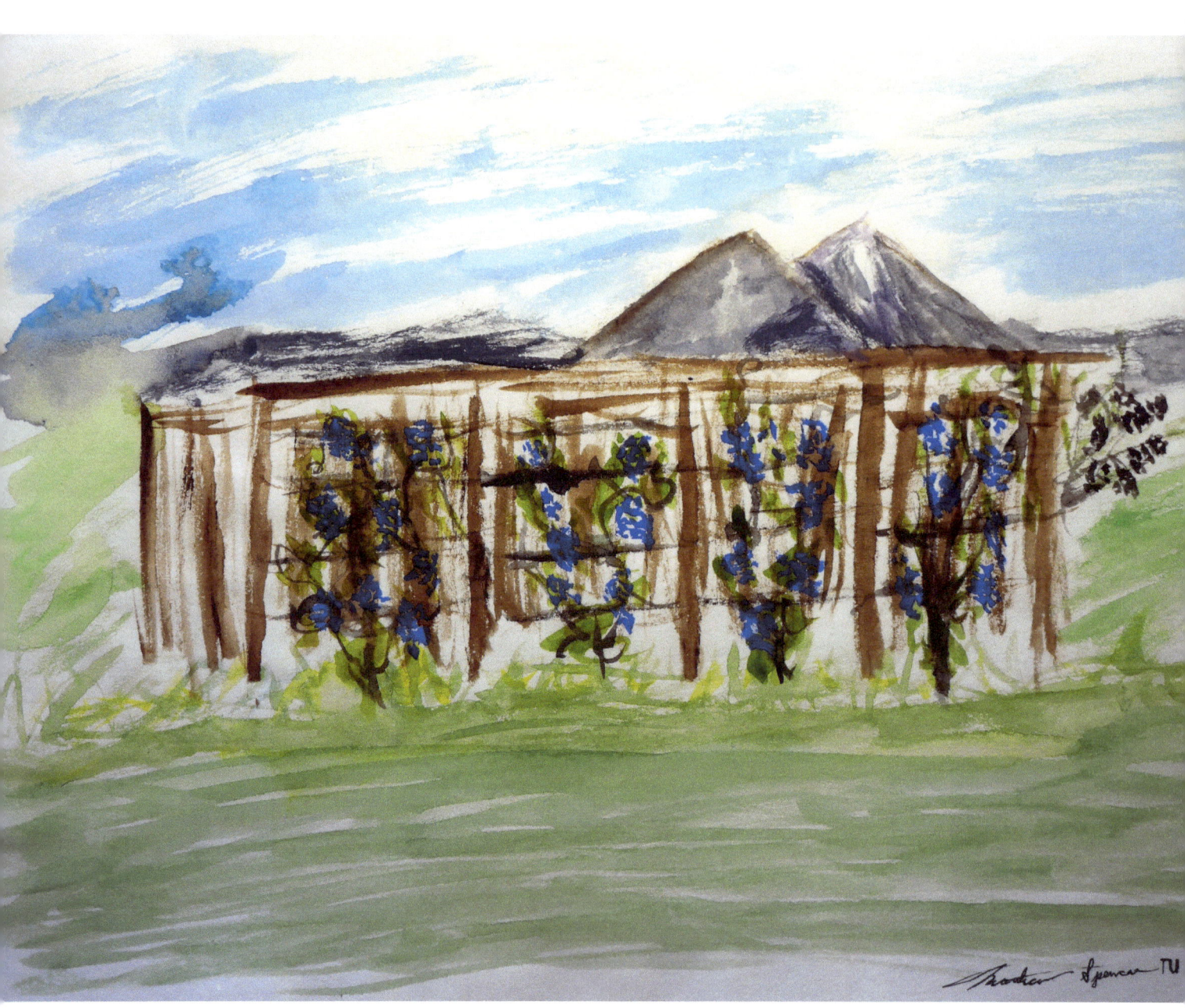

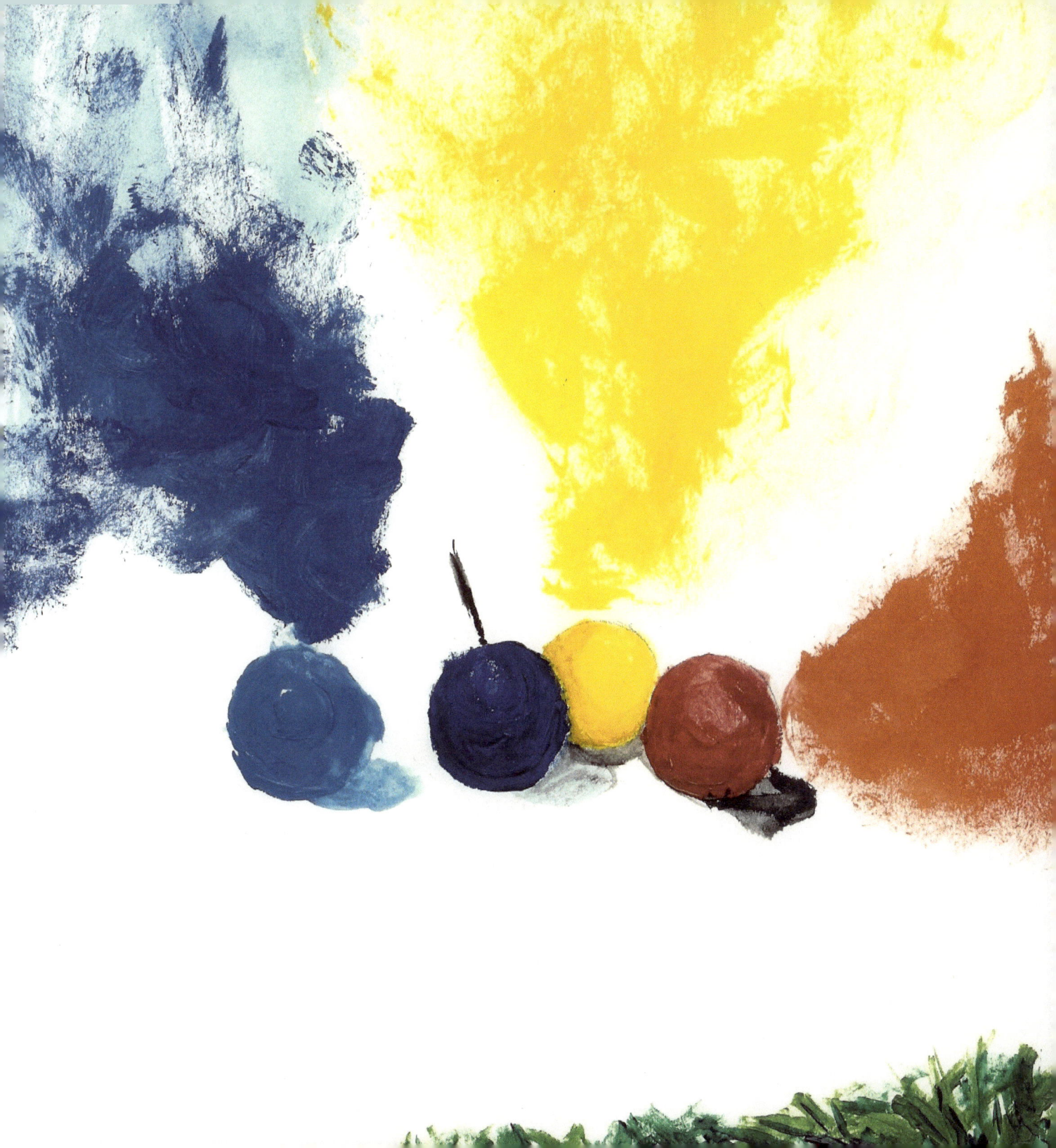

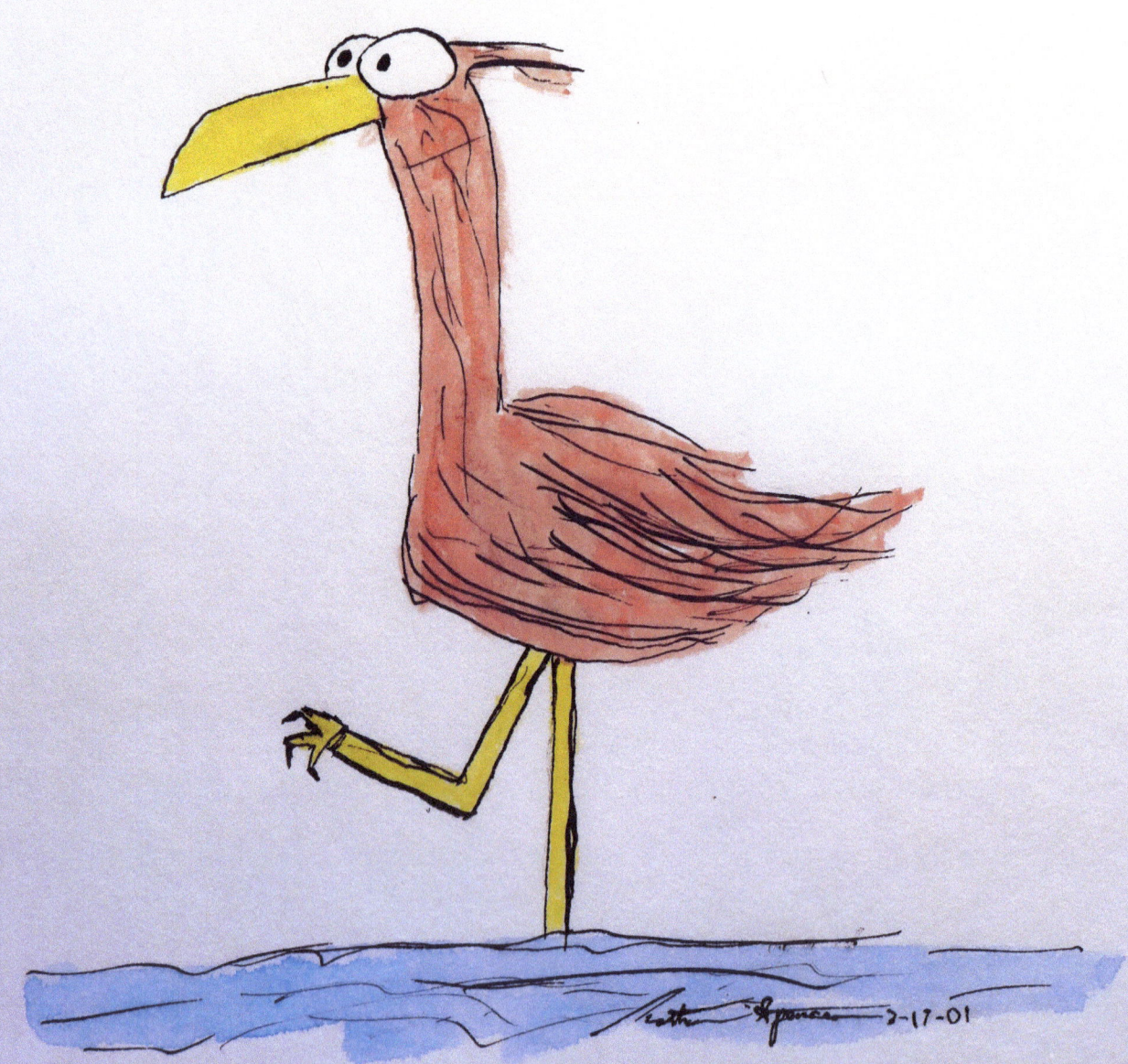

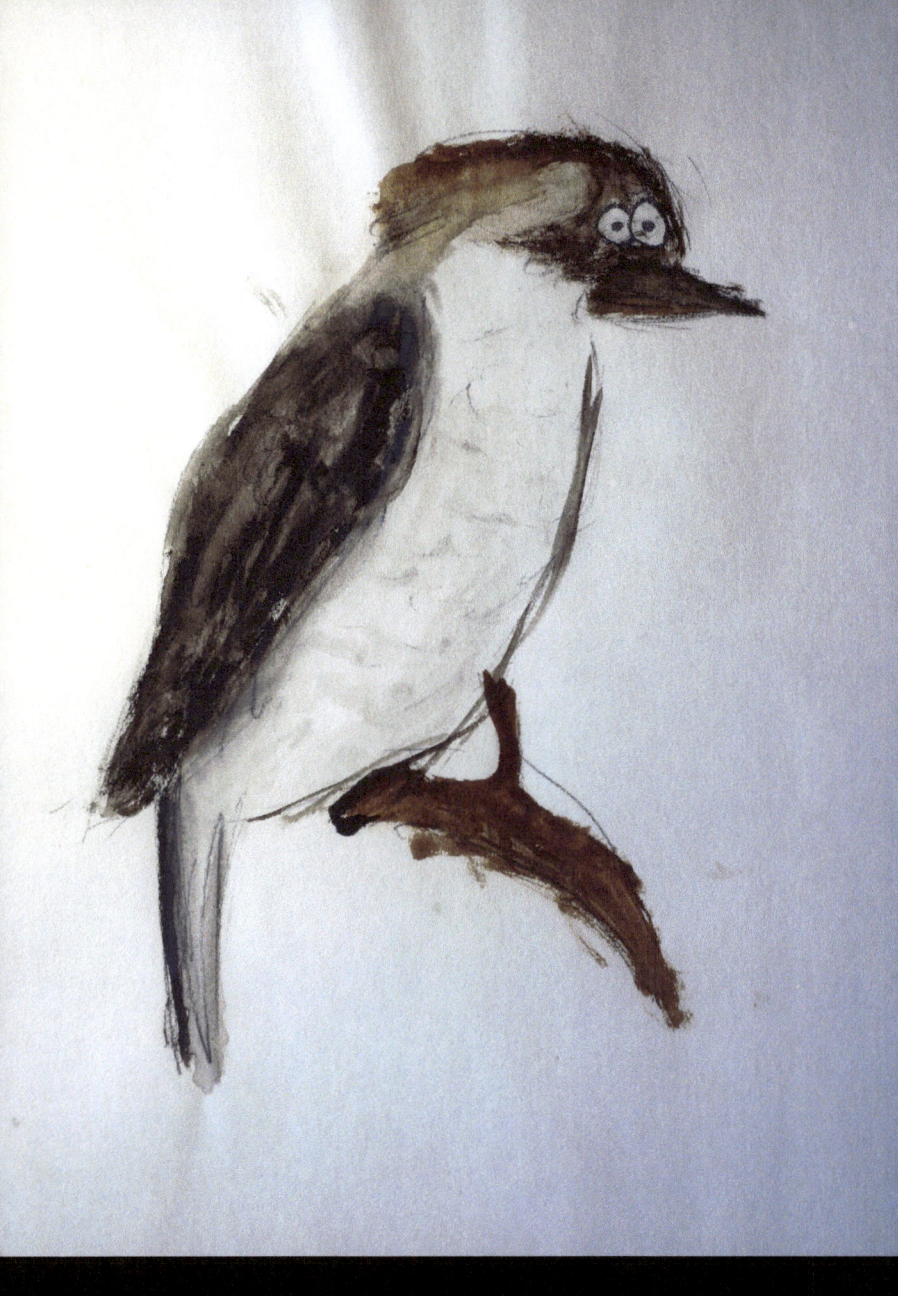

I love to draw cartoons…and Kookaburras!

Fantastic Worlds & Amazing Places

In the following pages, you will see images, colors, and shapes that evoke otherworldly landscapes, space travel, and adventure — past, present, and future!

Let the images tell the story!

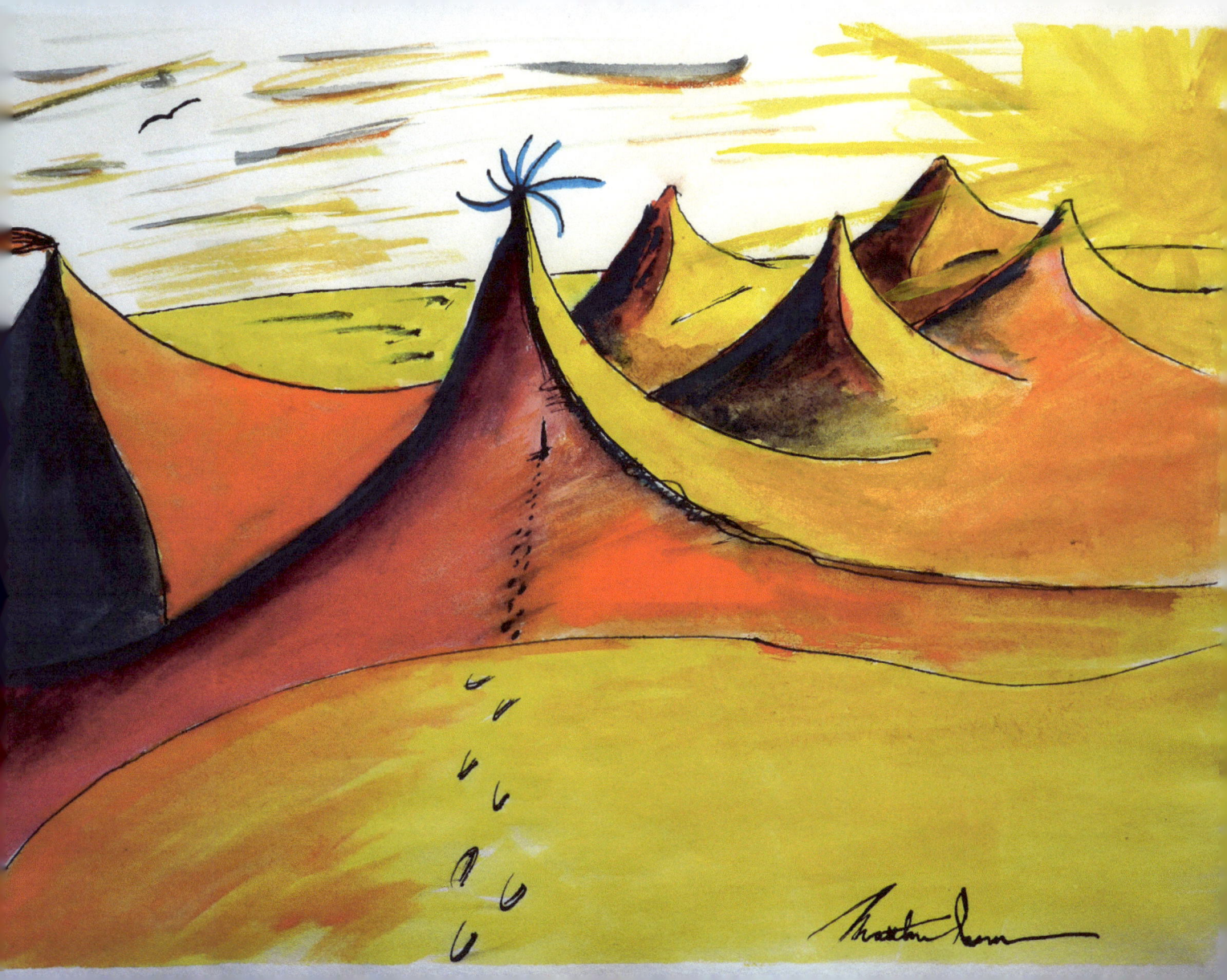

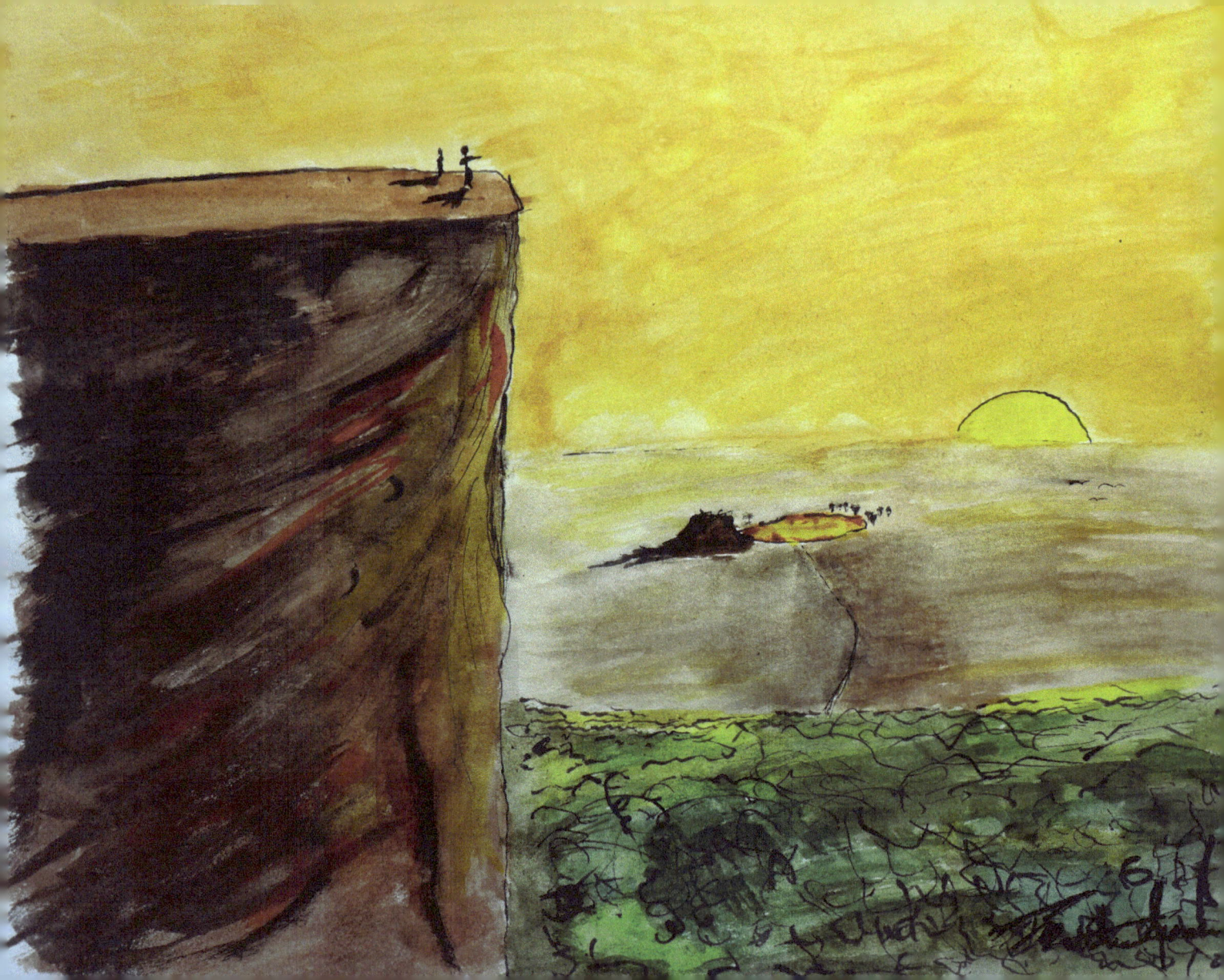

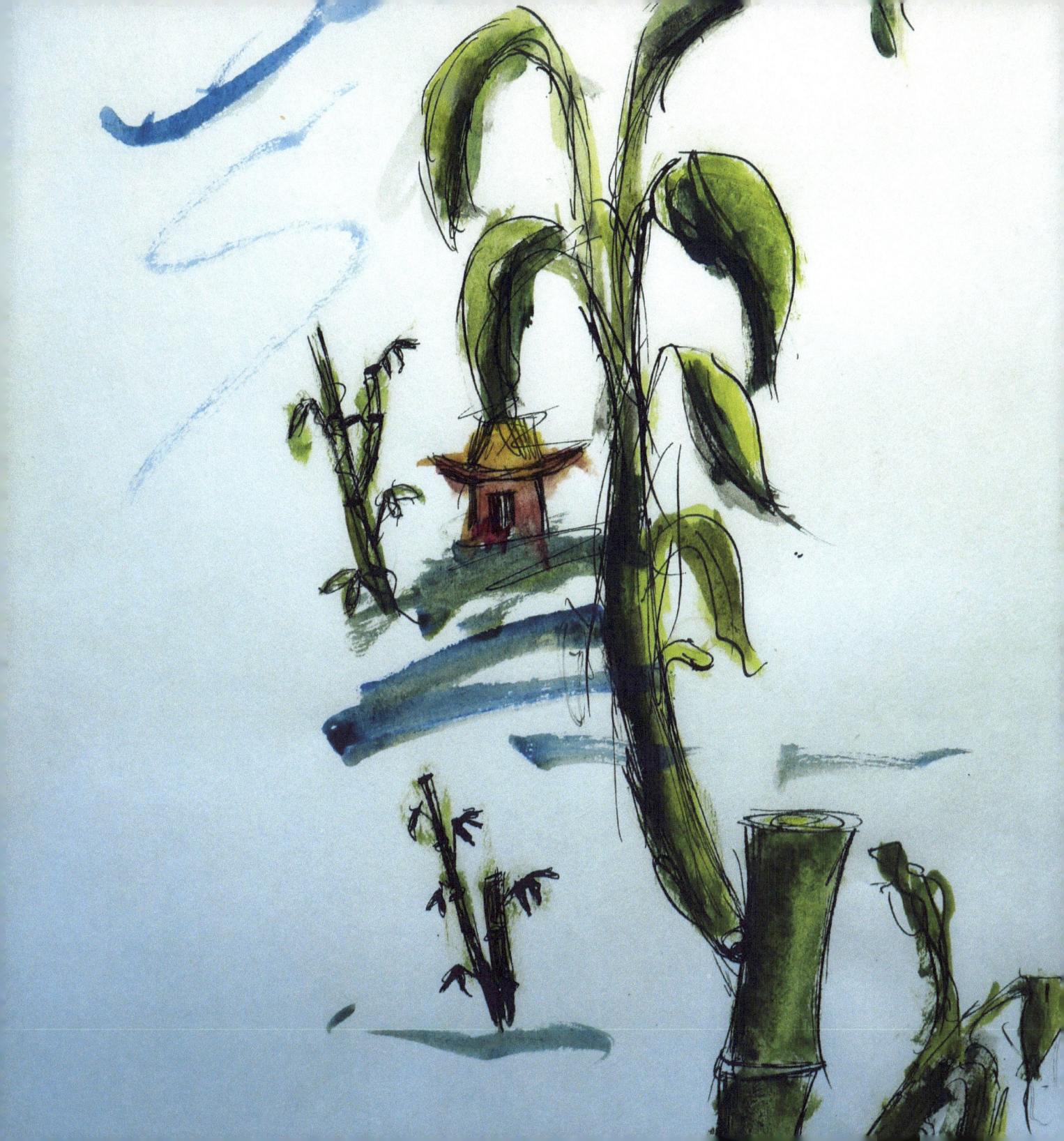

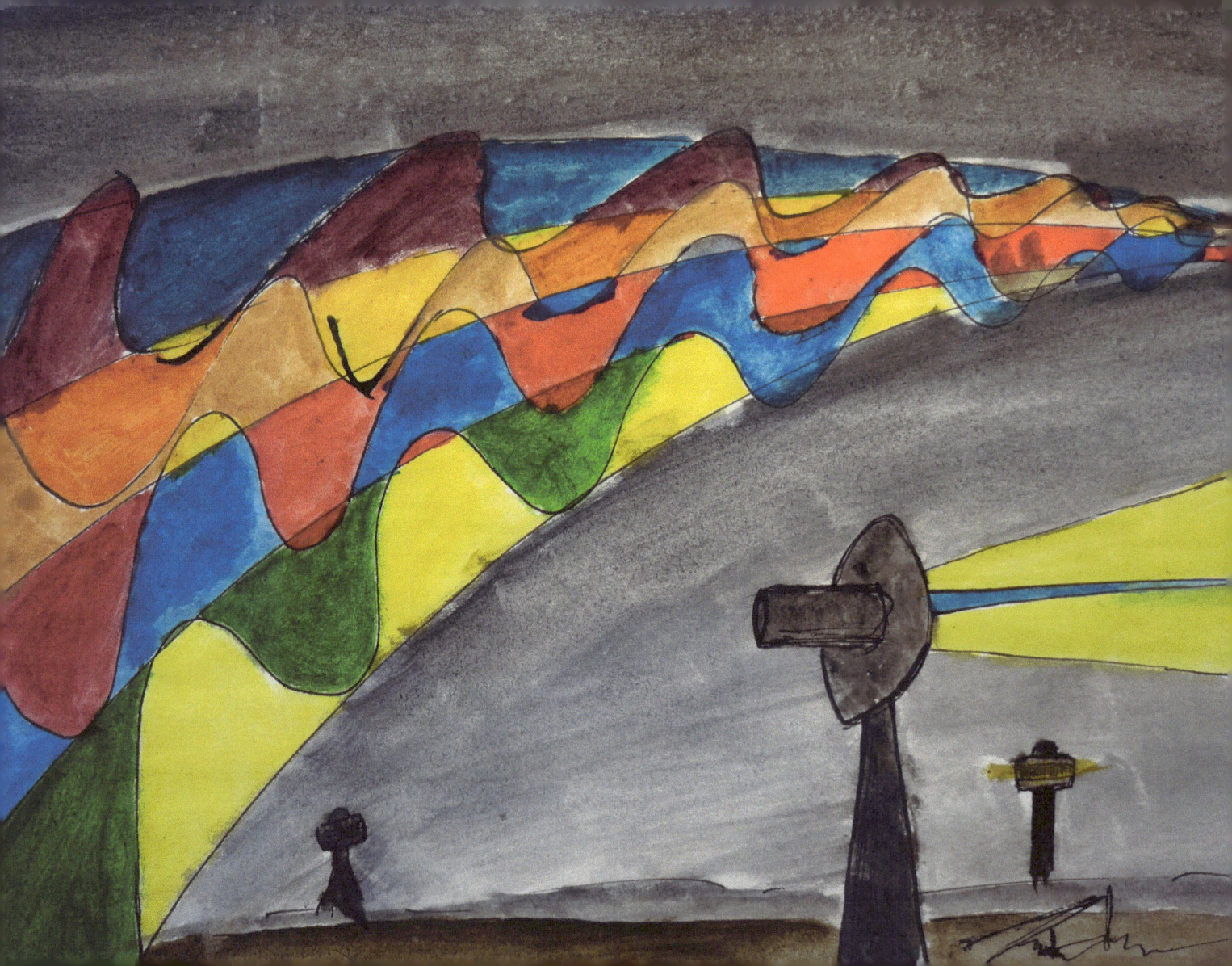

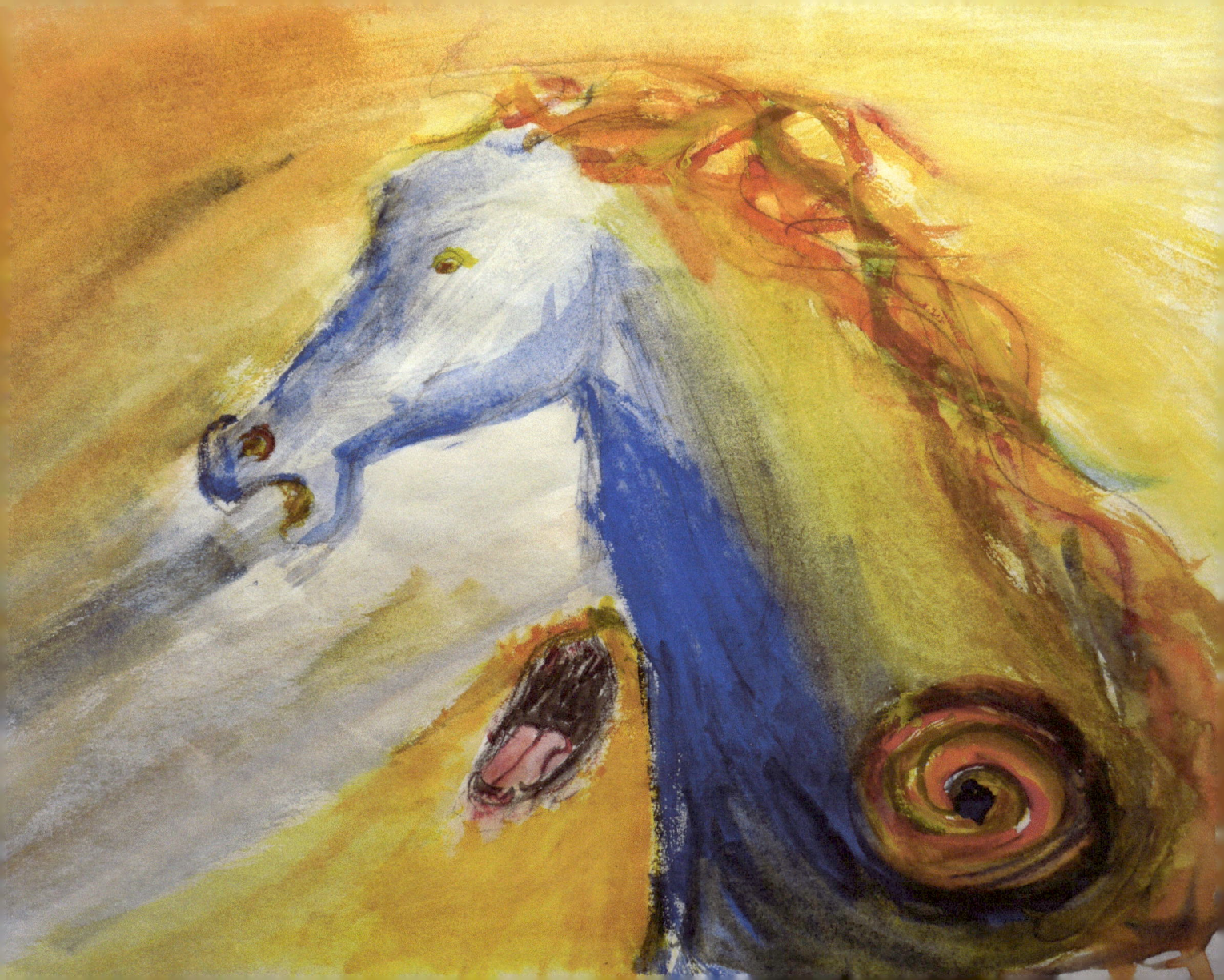

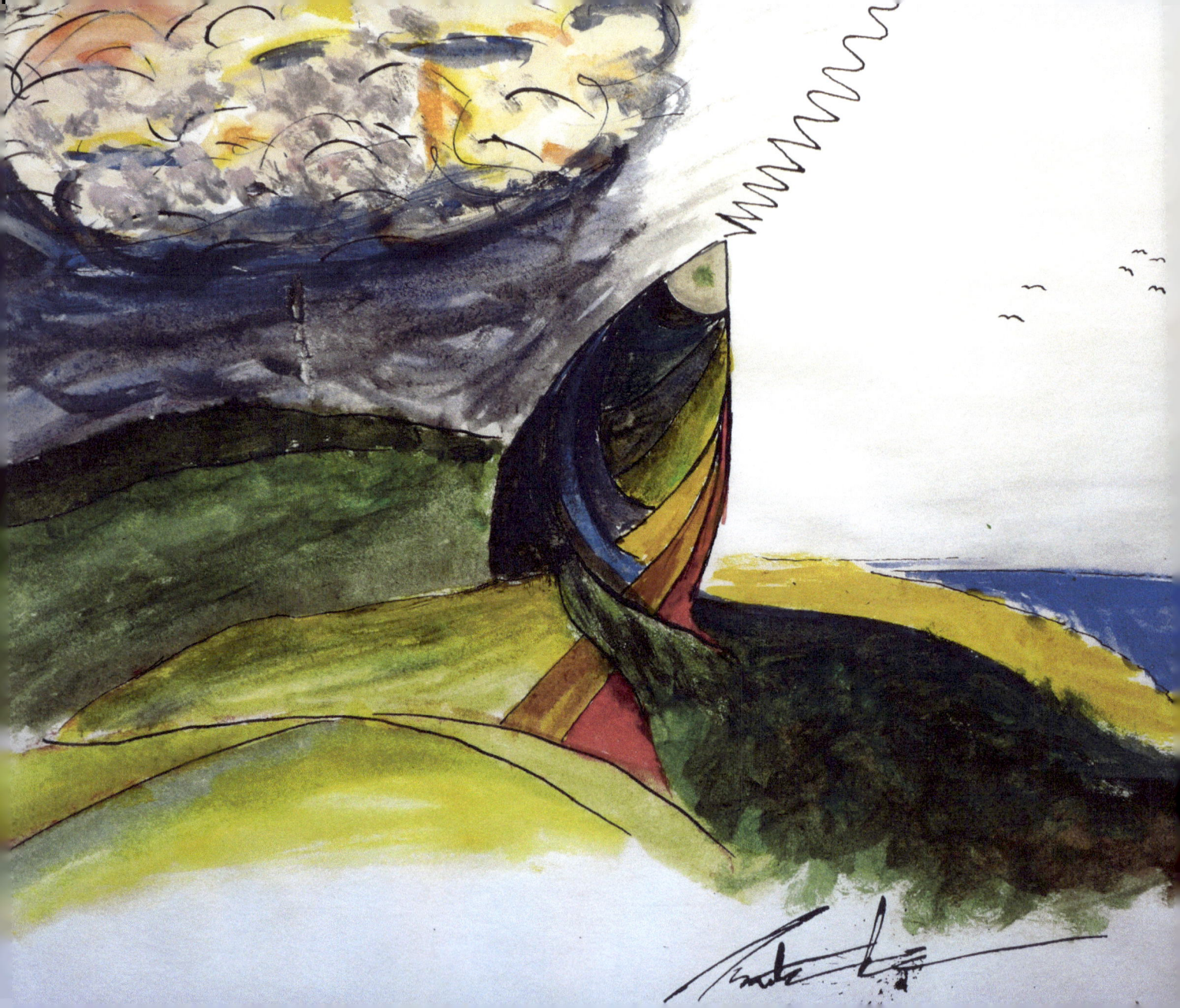

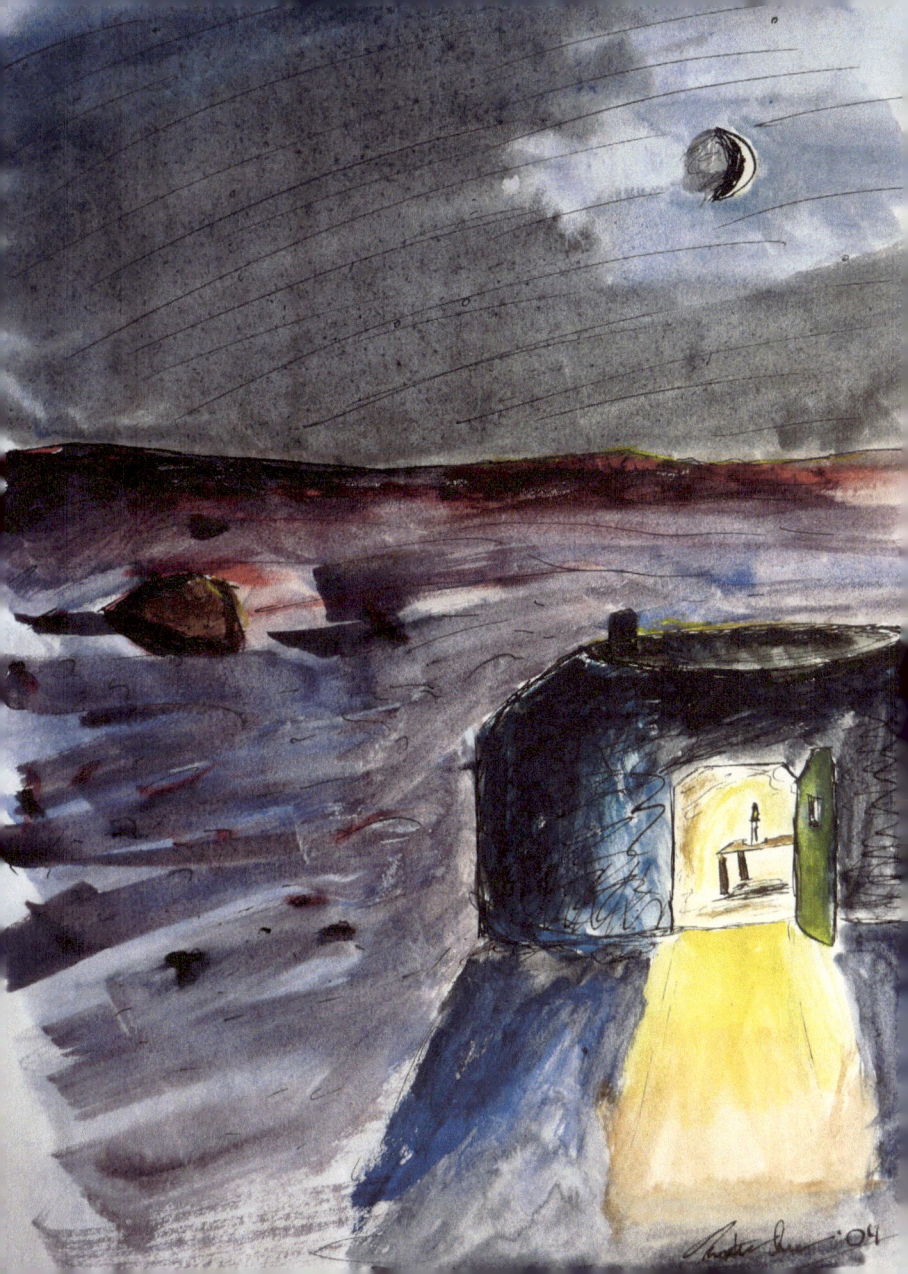

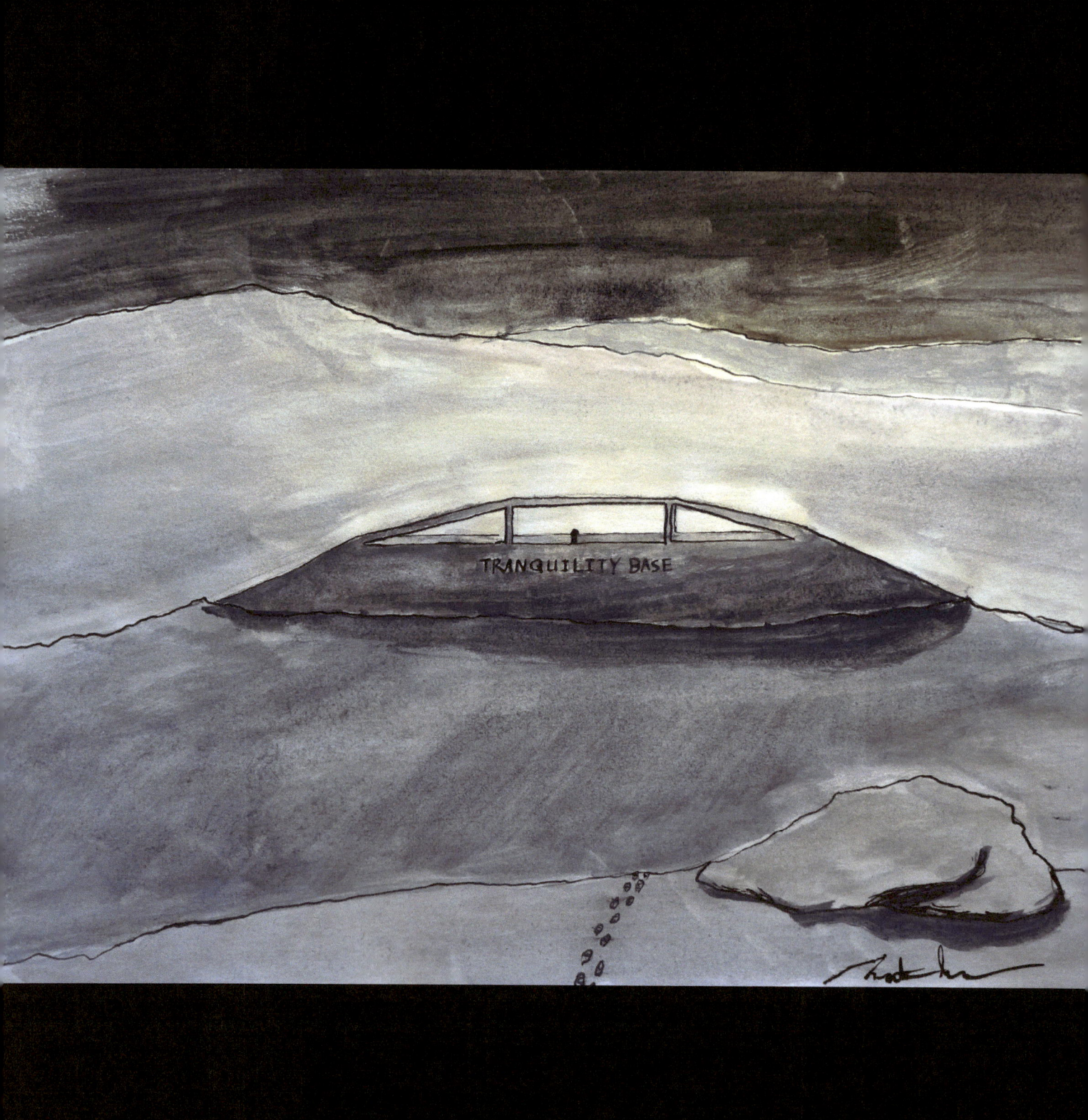

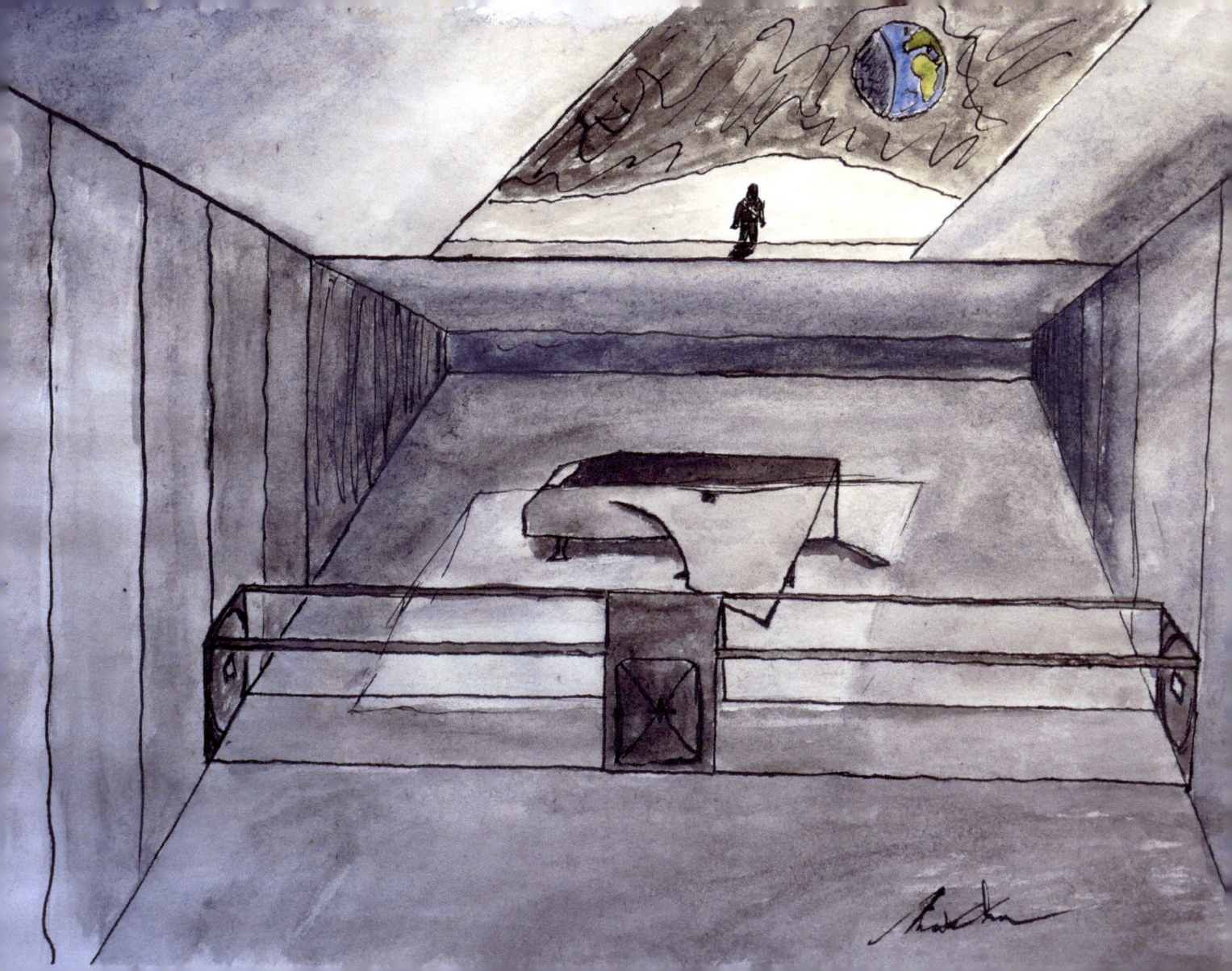

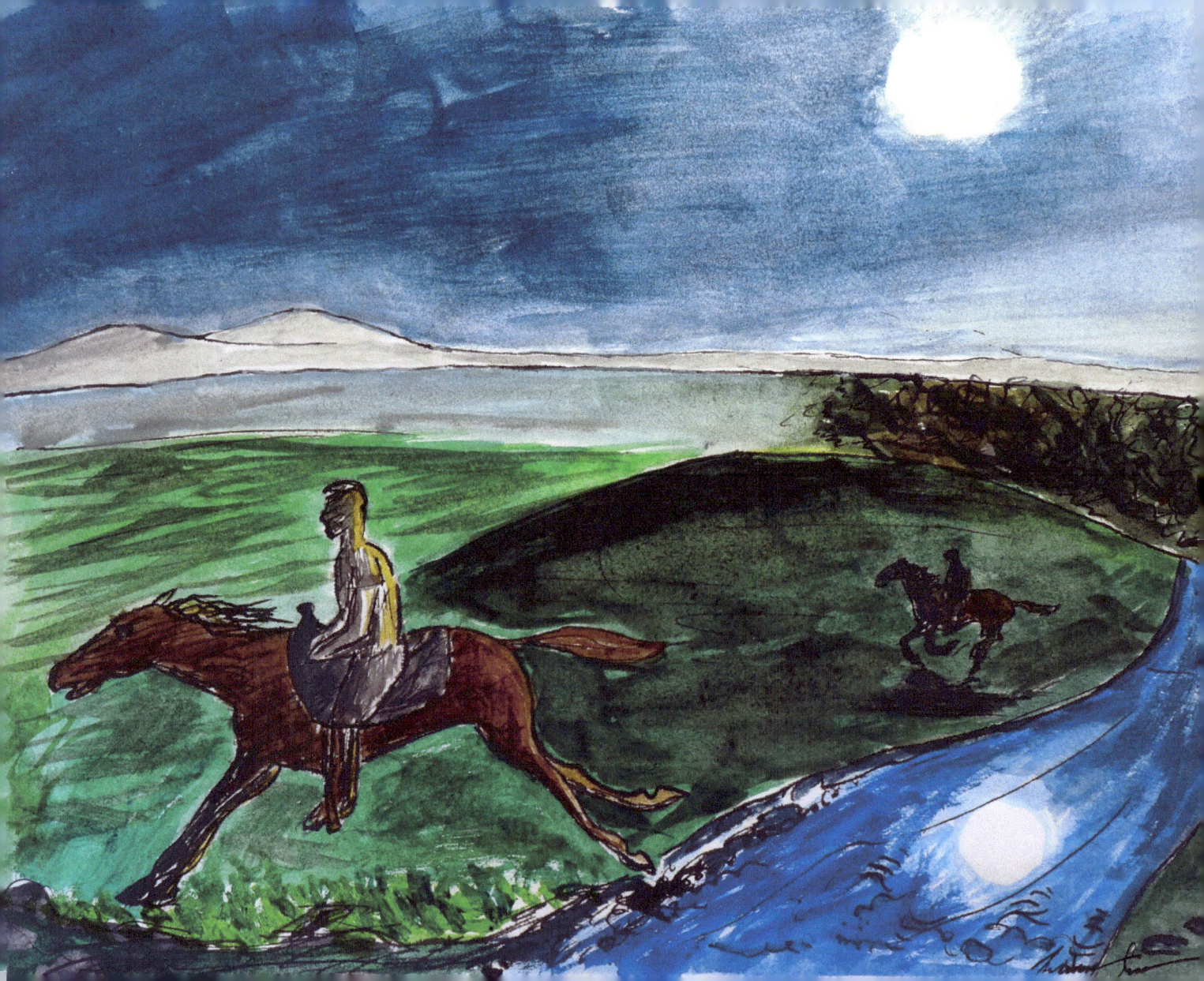

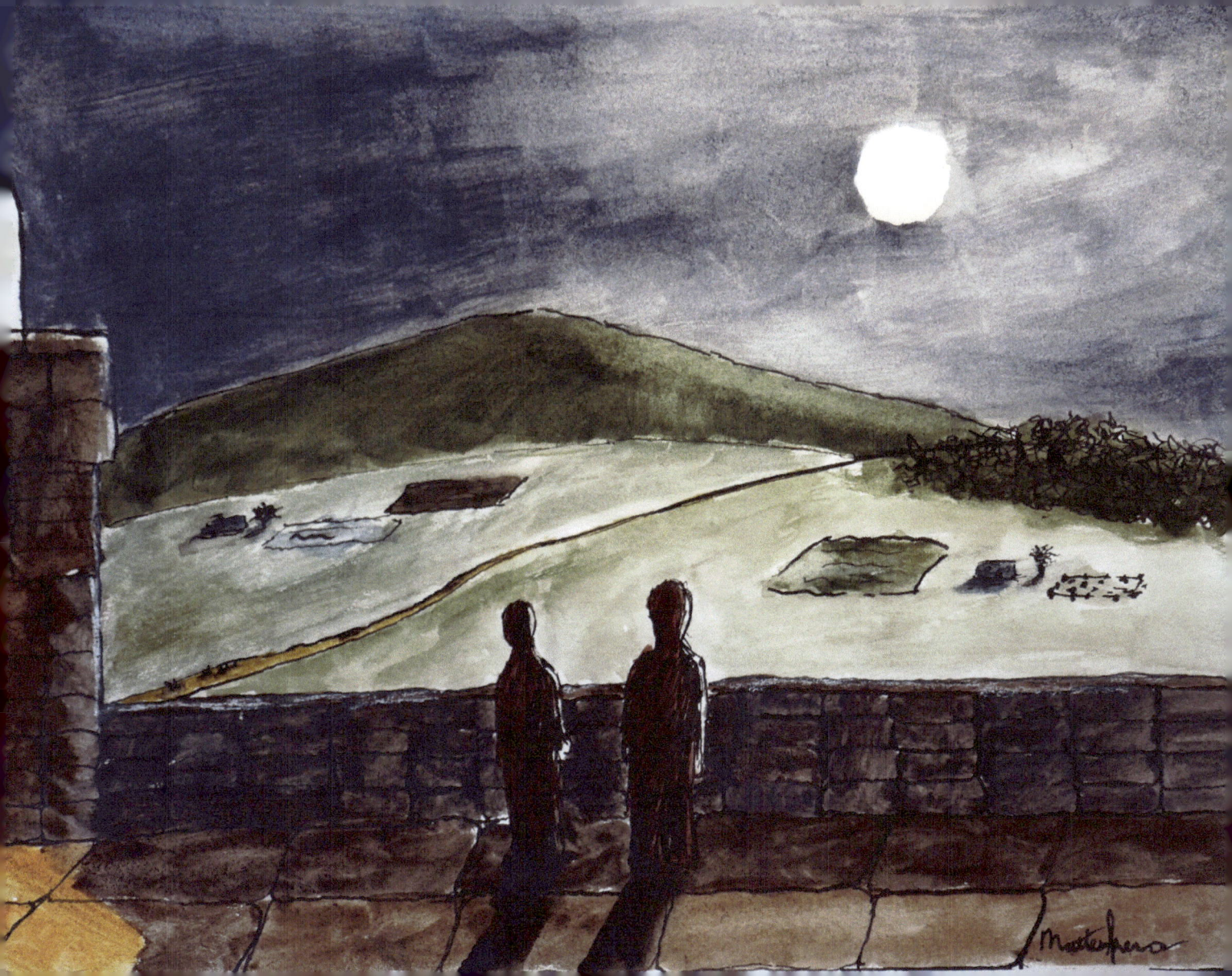

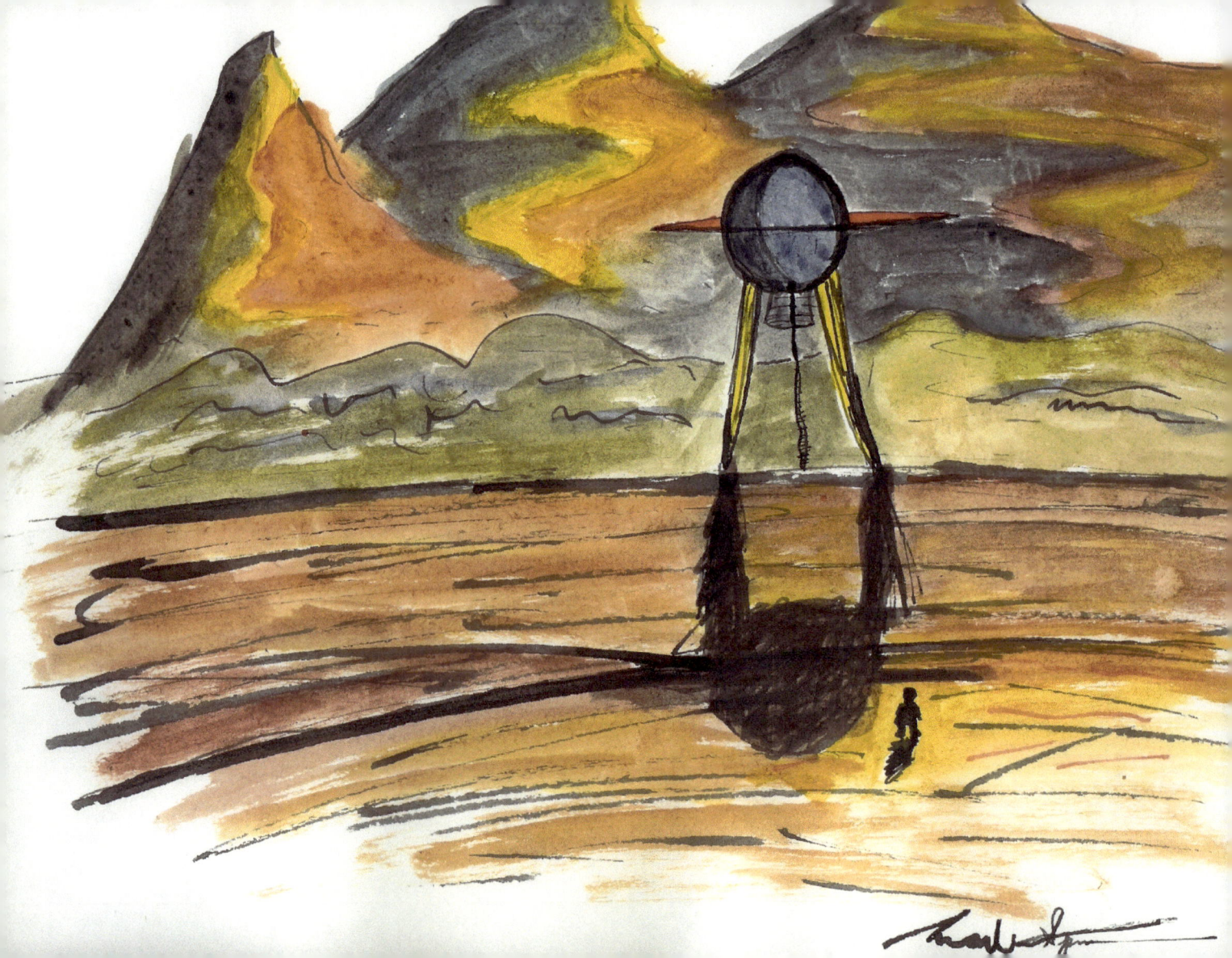

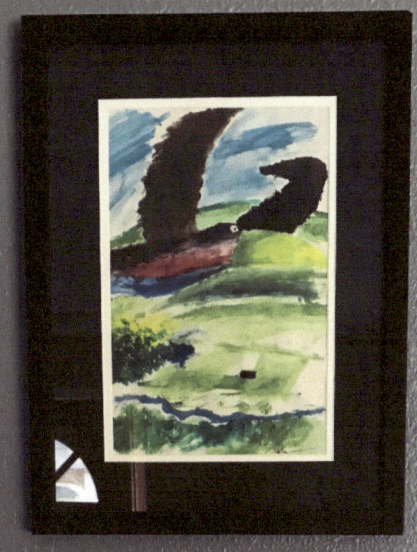
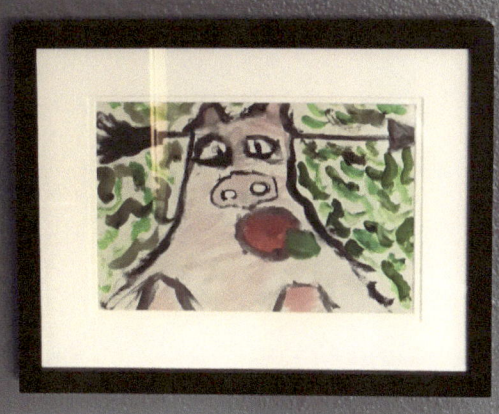

Courtesy of The Joshua Spencer Gallery

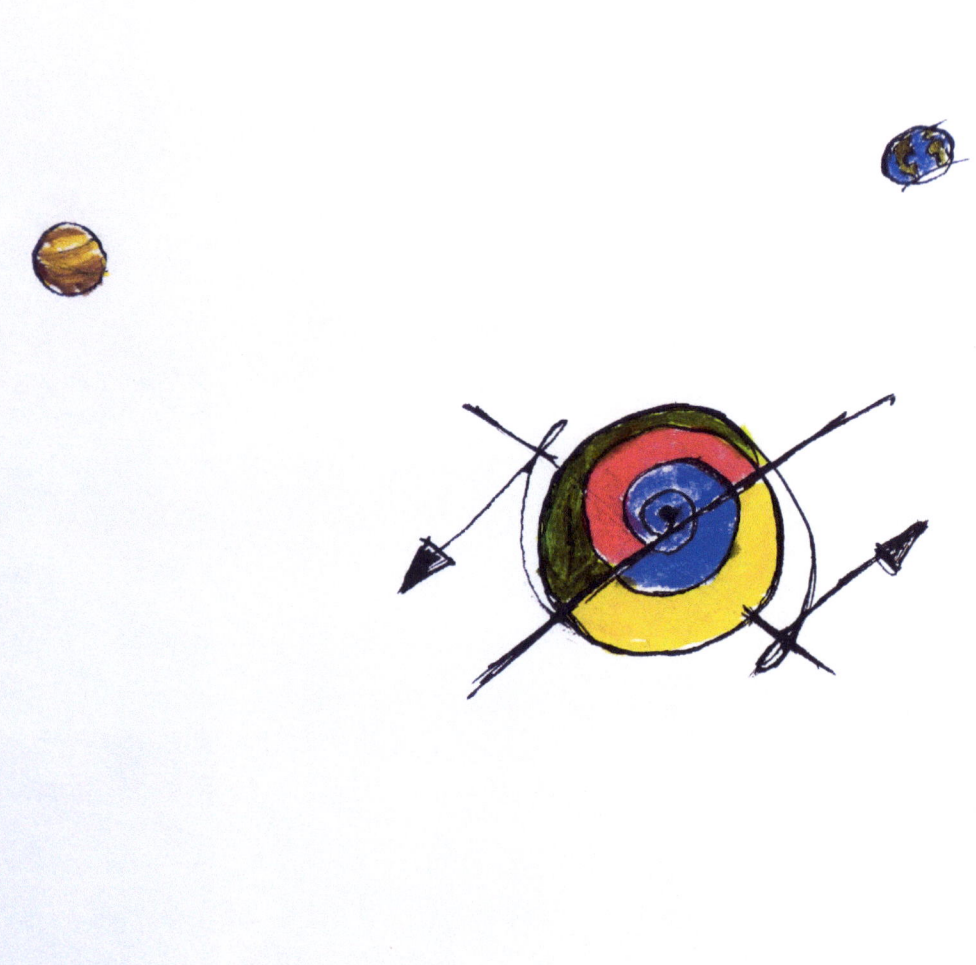

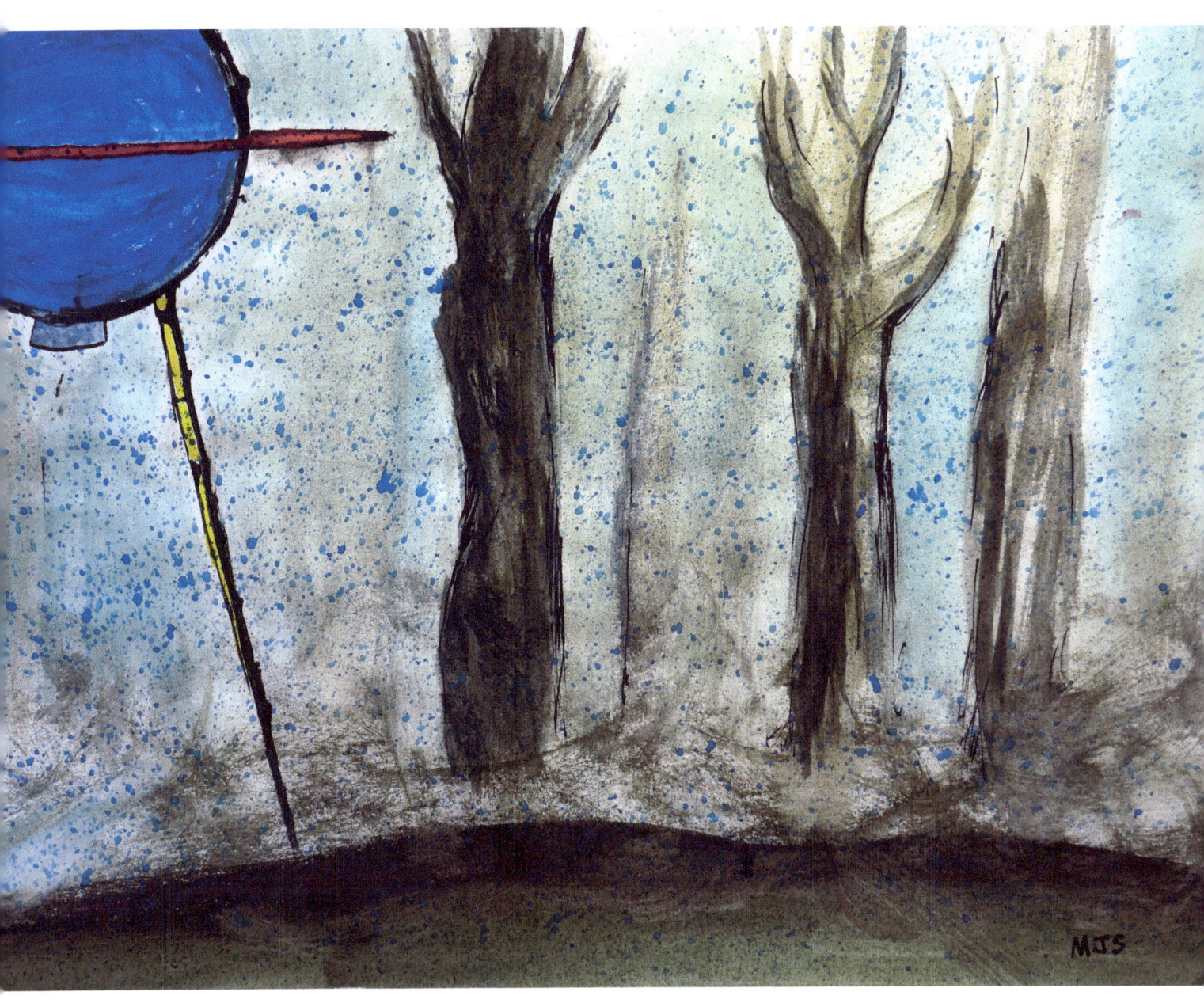

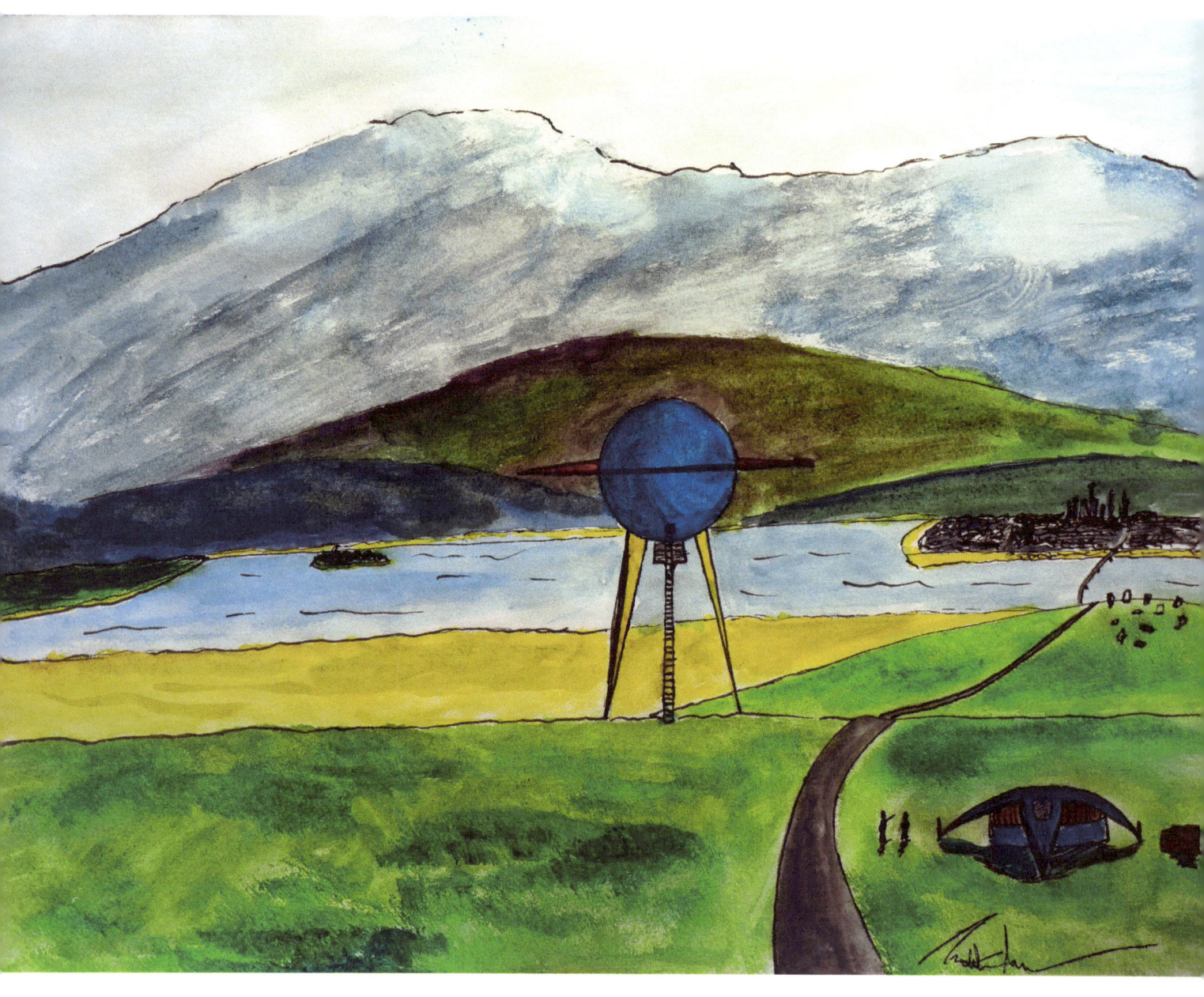

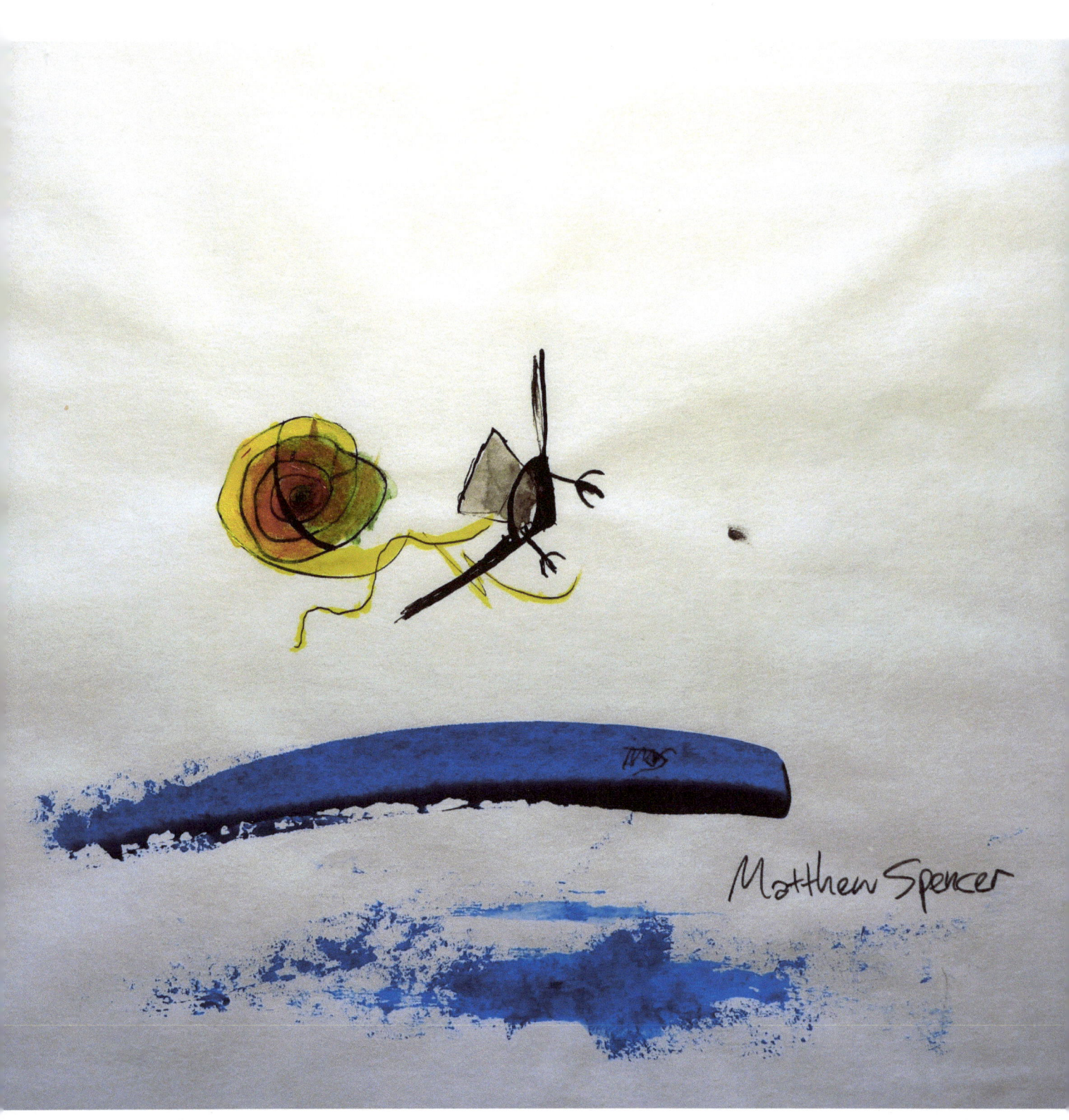

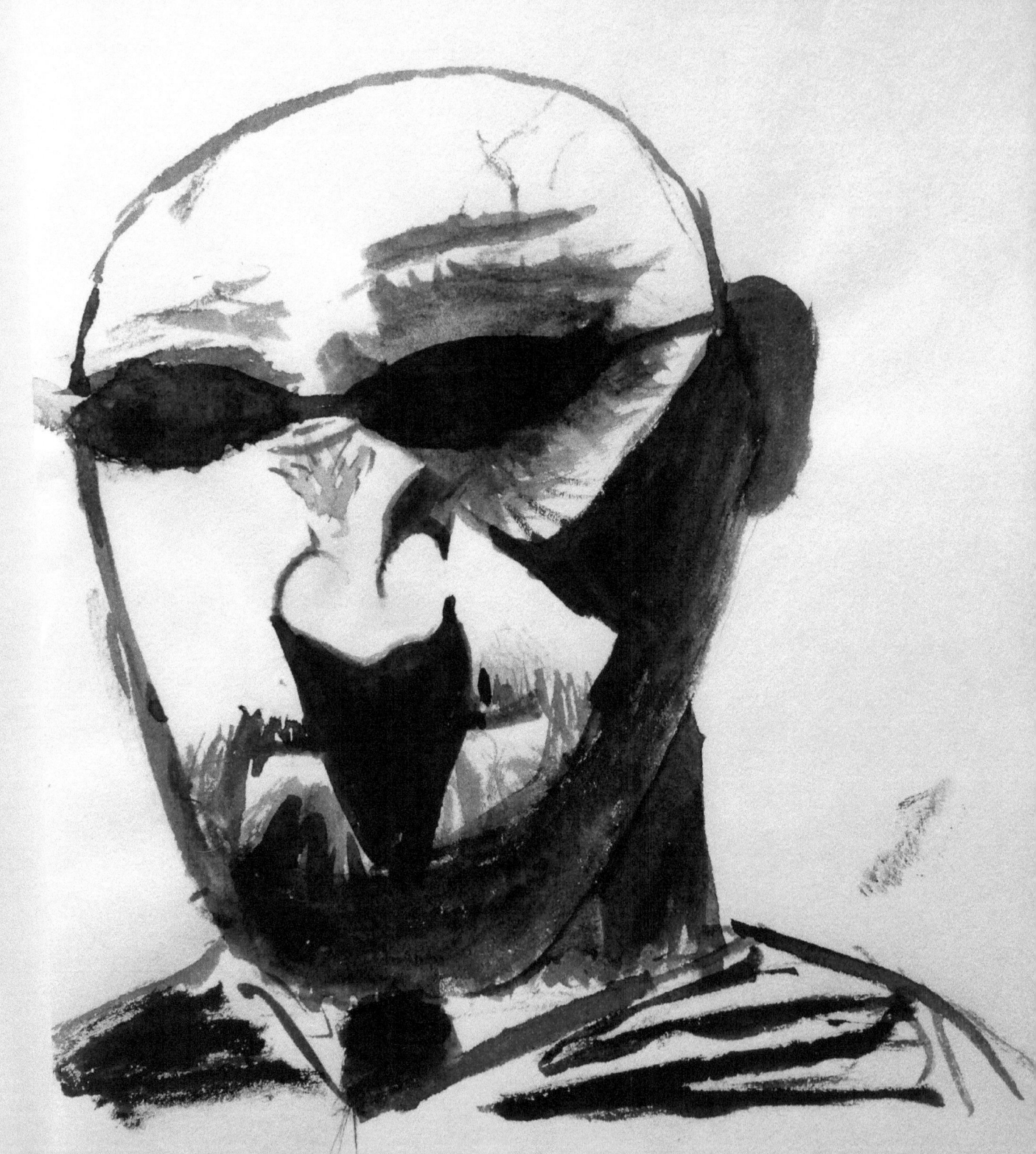

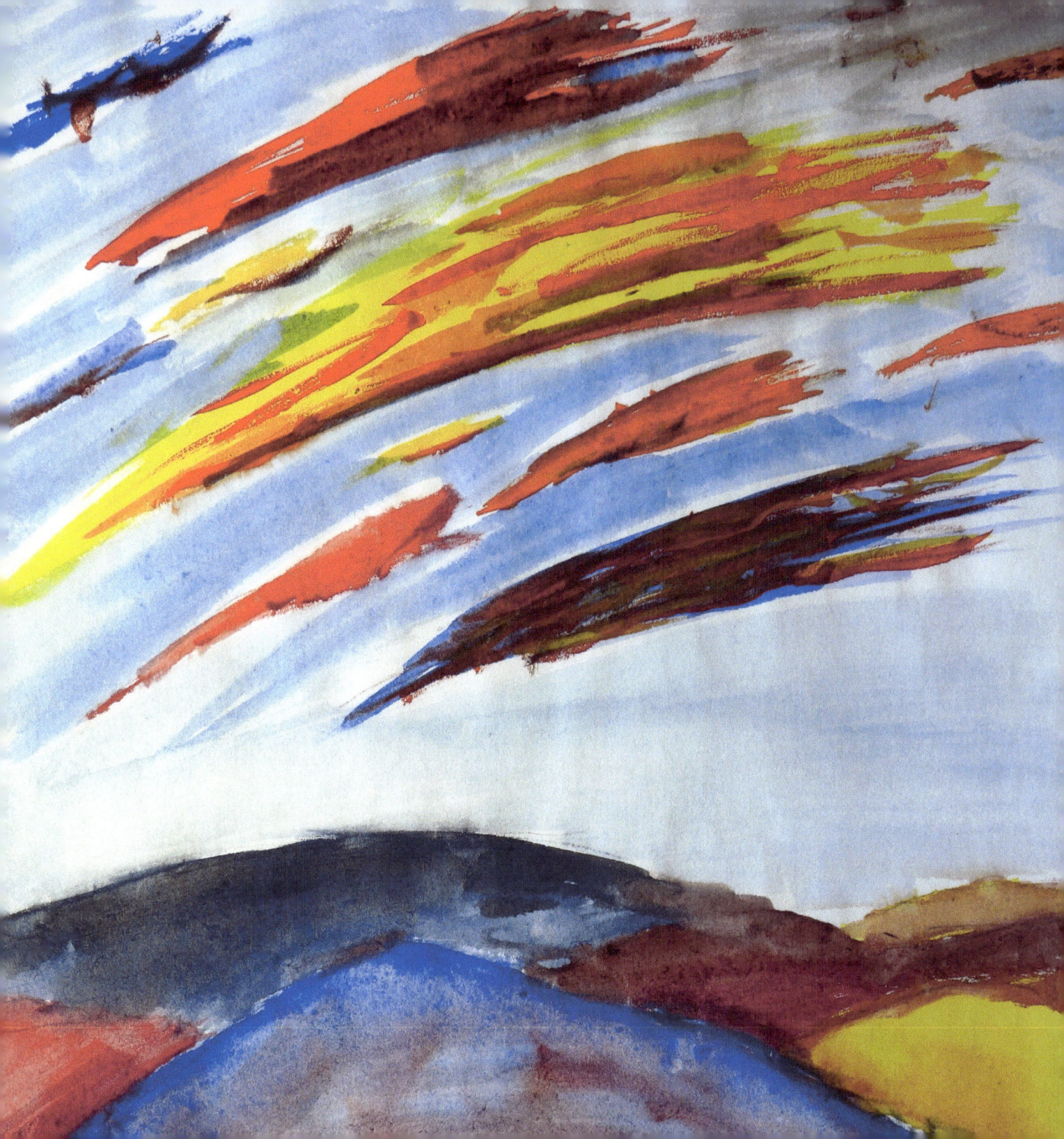

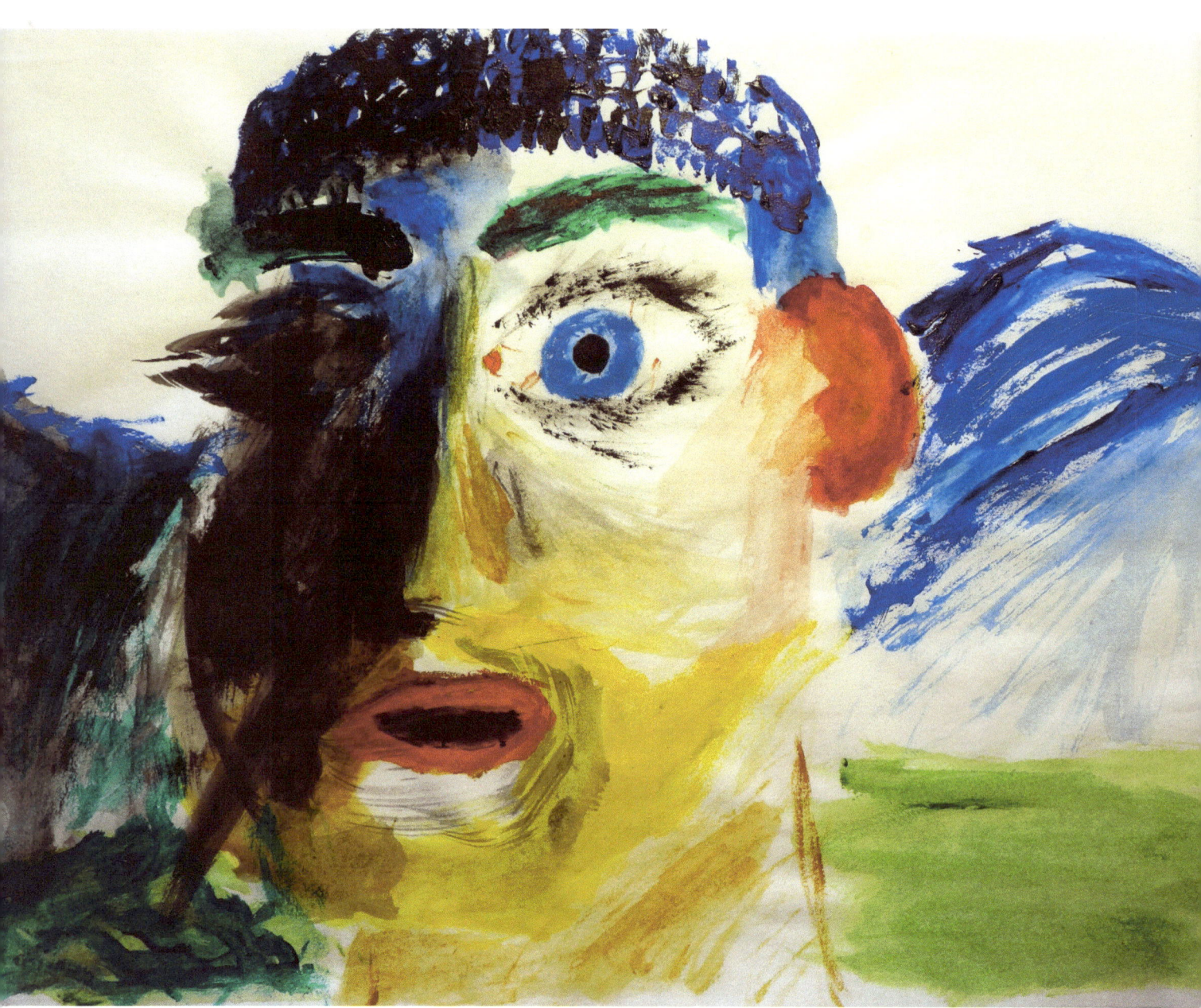

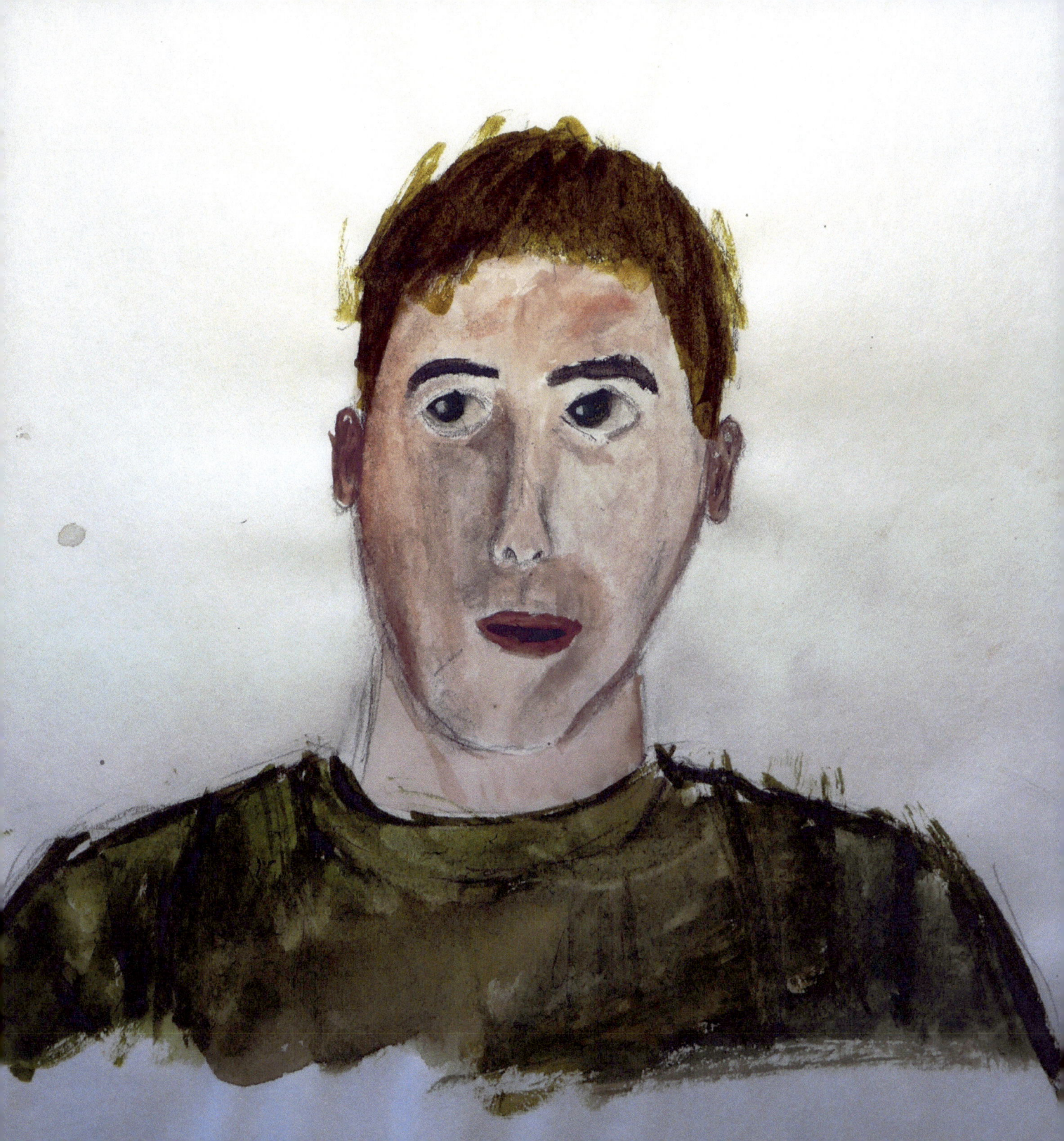

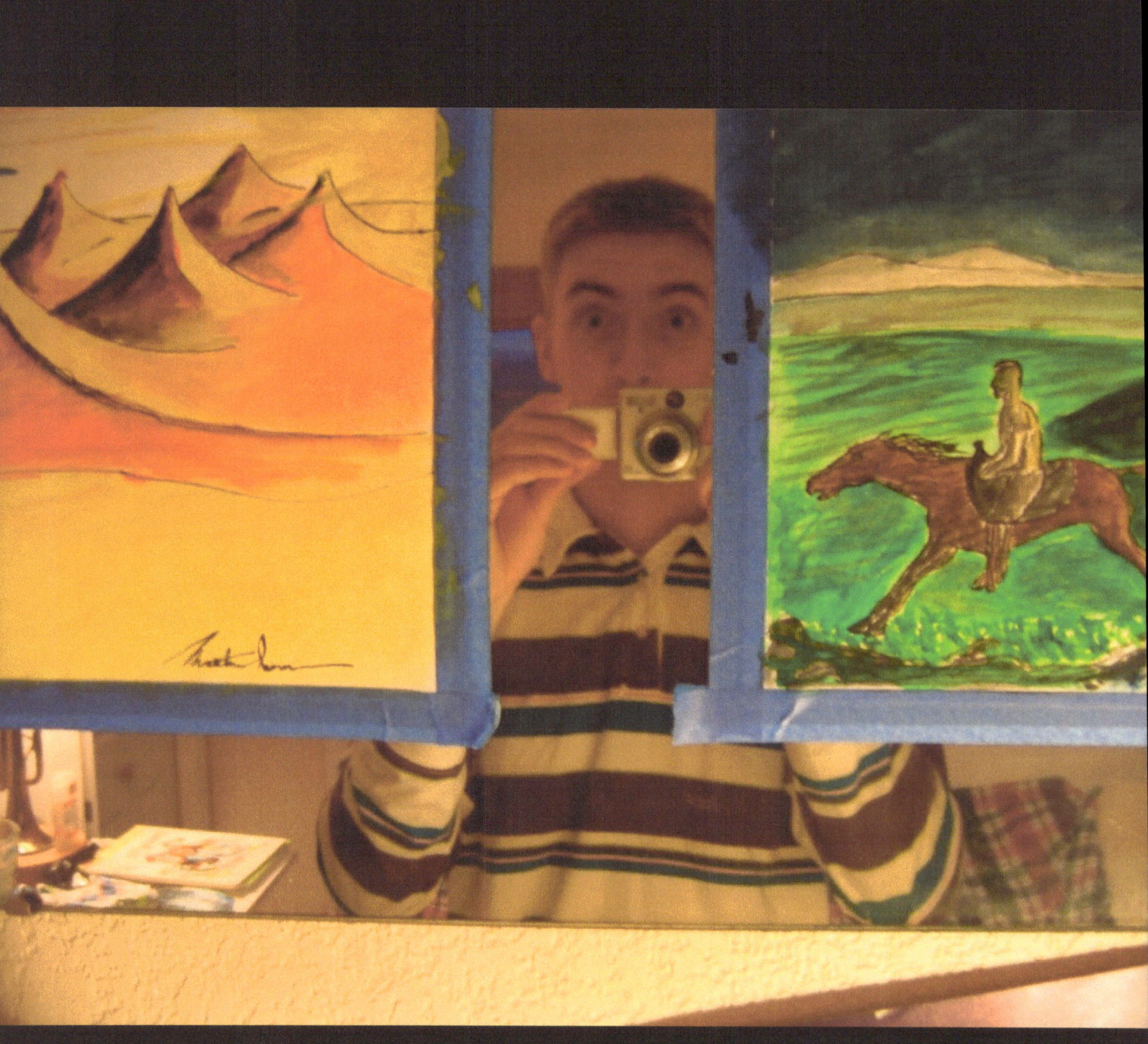

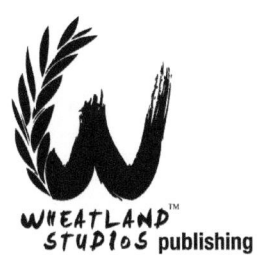